TAR

MW01222994

The Deep Sleep
That Awakens Your Dreams

DR. CRAIG JOHNSON
B.A., M.Div., D.Min.

Tardemah
The Deep Sleep That Awakens Your Dreams
ISBN 1-930027-19-2

Copyright © 2000 by Craig Johnson
Published by: Insight Publishing Group
8801 South Yale, Suite 410
Tulsa, OK 74137

Cover design and production: Paragon Communications Group, Inc., Tulsa, OK

CONTENTS

FOR NORMA CHRIS

Haec...scripsi...non otii abundantia sed amoris erga te.

I have written these things out of the abundance,
not of my leisure, but of my love towards you.

Cicero E.P., Book 7, I.

ACKNOWLEDGEMENTS

I would like to thank everyone who helped in the preparation of this book. My family for their great patience, the Saints and Shepherds Council of Bethel Christian Fellowship. Yet by far the greatest debt is owed to three extraordinary women:

BETTY O'NEAL—My beloved friend, secretary, and co-laborer in the ministry these 20 years.

LINDA STANLEY—You are a light to all who have the privilege of knowing you. Without your one hundred percent support this book could never have been completed! Thank you.

CARRIE LANGSAM—What a blessing you are. Thank you for believing in us and taking such good care of Michael.

FOREWORD

Are you too wide-awake to dream? Did you know that when God comes to fulfill His greatest promises He often first puts us to sleep? We will discover that divine sleep alone can produce some of the greatest healing, delivering, and restorative works in our lives.

This book was born out of a great personal struggle in my own life, a place where I had to learn that only the God of Adam, Abraham and Jacob could determine the hour of my final deliverance.

There are many times in life, when after "having done all," we must simply "stand" as we await the final touch from heaven that will complete God's work in us. Such a sovereign visitation is known in the Bible by the Hebrew word *tardemah*!

We will examine three instances of *tardemah* in the Scriptures. In each case the people we'll study had done all that they could do to deliver themselves, yet only a sovereign intervention of divine sleep would fulfill their deepest longings. These three *tardemahs* are soon to come upon the entire world! Throughout redemptive history, God has put His servants to sleep in order to make their dreams come true. It is my prayer that wherever you are in God's redemptive dealings, you might remember that He has a plan, whether you presently see it or not, and that affliction, though lasting, is not everlasting.

Craig Johnson
Agoura Hills, CA

INTRODUCTION

I have three passions in life. The first is to see God meet *impossible needs*! I long to see the truly broken of this world, from incest survivor to AIDS victim, gloriously healed. I dream of the traumatized, the hopeless and the helpless, those usually relegated to the back of the Revival Tent, being brought forth front and center and completely delivered!

As with *Adam,* I pray that God will soon bring a "sleep-like' visitation to all those plagued with unyielding bondages, that He will perform all necessary surgery, and then walk a complete fulfillment into their lives!

My second passion is to see God pour out His glory and power in the *reconfirmation* of *impossible destinies.* I believe this to be a generation unparalleled in human history. It will be impossible to "pull in the net" of revival apart from a fresh *reconfirmation* and *empowerment* of the "life words" God has given each of His children alive today.

Hundreds of millions in our time are destined to see, in one generation, spiritual offspring as numberless as the *stars of the heavens* and the *sands of the sea.* Many whose lives are extraordinarily significant have been feeling *old, tired,* and *barren.* To these, God is about to bring thunderous *reaffirmation* and a new release of His presence. Many will soon "sleep" as did *Abraham*, so that God might *reconfirm* and *fulfill* the "life words" He has given.

My third passion is to see God bring a complete restoration to the vast army of the "fallen." There are countless "leaders and followers" of Christ who bear the stigma of an *unredeemed past.* Many saints from every background and gifting as a result of "willful disobedience and moral failure," have condemned themselves to long sentences in the "prisons of God."

I believe a *twenty-year statute of limitations* on certain sins and their penalties is up! God's prisoners may yet be superficially bound in their "grave clothes," but they are surely not forgotten. *"The sighing of the prisoner has come before him ... He will preserve even those appointed to death."* (Ps. 79:11)

God will soon revisit His captives in order to "commute" *life sentences.* God will soon grant a gracious "sleep of visitation" similar to that which came upon *Jacob,* so that He might *utterly restore* what, to men, appears *unrestorable!*

The three *tardemahs* we'll study answer the three passions articulated above. They are *yet future,* and I for one have no idea how to hasten their day! I offer the following pages in the hope that, through them, God might revive your own desire to "seek Him."

The imagery we'll encounter of God, tenderly putting His little ones to *sleep* in order to make their dreams come true, is a deeply moving one for me. The *tardemahs* we'll study involve "actual sleep," yet we will widen their application to embrace "seasons of visitation," which nonetheless, yield similar fruit to that produced in *Adam, Abraham* and *Jacob.*

The three men whose "sleep life" we'll examine neither *expected, sought* nor *felt worthy* of their respective *tardemah* visitations. *Tardemah seasons* come as do dreams. They are *uncoerced, untimed,* yet *undeniable.*

This book is dedicated to *you,* "God's chosen," and to the honor of the One:

"Who delivered us from so great a death, and doth deliver; in whom we trust that He will yet deliver us." (II Corinthians 1:10)

Craig Johnson

CHAPTER ONE

The Higher Ministries of Sleep

"Now while he was talking with me, I sank into a deep sleep with my face to the ground; but he touched me and made me stand upright." (Dan. 8:18)

There is a Hebrew word that appears frequently in the Holy Scriptures. It is pronounced *tar-day-ma*. It is a word used on occasion to describe simple sleep, but most frequently it speaks of instances of sovereign intervention, redemptive acts so significant that a life can sometimes only be understood in terms of BT (before *tardemah*) and AT (after *tardemah*).

TARDEMAH: WHAT THE SCHOLARS SAY
The following are a few quotations that might help us to better understand what *tardemah* truly means:

"A deep sleep produced by God," (Keil and Delitzsche).

"A coma like state often caused by God, making an individual insensible to things around him." (Expository Dictionary of Bible Words)

"A God-given trance which opens the mind to revelation and ecstasy." (Interpreters Commentary on the Bible)

"The profundity of divine intervention, it is God who casts such sleep... upon his chosen servant." (Theological Workbook of the Old Testament)

"Not a common sleep through weariness or carelessness, but a divine ecstasy, the doors of the body are locked up, that the soul might be private and retired, and might act more freely." (Matthew Henry)

We will discover that God both speaks and acts in strategic ways through "seasons" of divine sleep. The *tardemahs* of which we speak are not mere physical sleep, but rather "sleep-like" visitations which leave in their wake a transformed life!

GOD NEVER SLEEPS

The fact that God ministers to His servants through sleep shouldn't surprise us for the Scriptures teach that God uses sleep in incredibly creative ways:

"It is vain for you to rise up early, to retire late, to eat the bread of painful labors; for he gives to his beloved even in his sleep." (Ps. 127:2).

The above verse teaches that God *gives* to us in the night seasons, even when all our faculties are shut up from waking realities.

Dick Mills points out:

"This word from Psalm127:2 stresses that He is continuously giving even while we are asleep. The Good News Bible translates this verse by saying, *"the Lord provides for those He loves while they are asleep."*

One writer stated that, "God works when men do not work at all. He blesses and prospers them without any effort on their part." The Amplified Bible sums it all up:

"He gives (blessings) to his beloved in (their) sleep."

James Moffatt adds:

"God's gifts come to his loved ones while they sleep" (*A Word In Season, Vol. I,* Pg. 153, 1986, Dick Mills).

SLEEP AS A SYMBOL

The posture of sleep itself bespeaks a vulnerability and accessibility often used by God for *prophetic ends*. Job 33:15-17 describes God as working:

"In a dream, in a vision of the night, when sound sleep falls on men, while they slumber in their beds, then He opens the ears of men, and seals their instruction, that He

may turn man aside from his conduct, and keep man from pride."

Throughout Scripture *divine revelations* are also associated with the reality of deep sleep:

"But I heard the sound of His words; and as soon as I heard the sound of His words, I fell into a deep sleep on my face, with my face to the ground." (Dan.10:9)

Who could forget this famous passage:

"And Joseph arose from his sleep, and did what the Angel of the Lord commanded him, and took her as his wife." (Matt.1:24)

God is even seen exercising *paternal protection* over His children by putting their enemies to sleep.

"So David took the spear and the jug of water from the side of Saul's head, and they went away, but no one saw or knew it, nor did any awake, for they were all asleep, because a sound sleep from the Lord had fallen on them." (I Sam. 26:12).

Acts 12:4-10, in the New Testament, records a miraculous deliverance of Peter from prison. This deliverance was also brought about through God-given slumber.

A SLEEP BEYOND SLEEP

Physical sleep can be understood as:

"The natural and temporary and periodical diminution of sensation, feeling, and thought amounting in heavy slumber to an almost complete cessation of conscious life."

The *tardemah* visitations we will speak of are not reducible to physical sleep alone. They have a wider application. More than mere conscious desolation, a divine *tardemah* equals a visitation of God by which a waking and watchful heart is transformed and delivered by the power of God!

11

SLEEP AND FAITH ARE UNIVERSAL

Another reason God uses images of sleep to instruct us is because the reality of sleep is universal. Each day this great power overwhelms the resistance of all men. All people daily, from the most wicked to the humblest saint, are reduced to this helpless state of much needed refreshment, rejuvenation, and dependency. Each day all of God's moral creation yields itself and its future to sleep. Is this not an excellent portrait of faith! Even the atheist surrenders to this mysterious unconsciousness in the hope that he will "rise again" the next morning and all will be new! All God requires of us is that we surrender consciously to Him at least as freely as we nightly yield to the realities of sleep!

Yet what about "seasons of divine sleep?" Do *tardemahs* come to us as frequently as nightly rest? Physical sleep comes to all of us, while divine sleep is more rare in its occurrences. *Tardemahs,* we'll discover, are unique "singularities", not repeatable "regularities". They are rare because they come *from* God and *only* when they are absolutely necessary. We cannot control them. We cannot bring them to others. We can only become willing candidates. Are you a candidate for a *tardemah?*

THREE INSTANCES OF *TARDEMAH*

We will examine three instances of *tardemah* in the Bible:

- Adam's *Tardemah* of Unknowing, (Gen. 2:21).
- Abraham's *Tardemah* of Divine Destiny, (Gen. 15:12).
- Jacob's *Tardemah* of Utter Grace, (Gen. 28:11).

In each example, God brings a deliverance of divine sleep to those seeking, hoping, and longing for spiritual transformation. Adam's deepest need will be identified and met; Abraham's impossible destiny will be reconfirmed; and Jacob's sinful past will be graciously redeemed.

Do you have a deep and abiding *unmet need?* Do you have a longing for a *reconfirmation* of God's promise regarding your future? Do you have anything in your past you need God to *fully redeem*? If so, then this book is for you!

THREE PROPHETIC WORDS FOR THE BODY OF CHRIST

After studying Adam's *Tardemah of Unknowing*, Abraham's *Tardemah of Divine Destiny*, and Jacob's *Tardemah of Utter Grace,* we will then apply these three truths "globally" to the next outpouring of the Holy Spirit. I believe the next move of God will be characterized as an outpouring of God's love and mercy embracing three areas of the human condition:

- *Impossible Needs* – Will be properly identified then met.
- *Impossible Destinies* – Will be reconfirmed with great power.
- *Impossible Pasts*– Will be redeemed as God restoratively addresses sin and its consequences!

In light of these facts I ask you again,
"ARE YOU TOO WIDE AWAKE TO DREAM?"

CHAPTER TWO

The *Tardemah* of Unknowing

"Everything out of which something new is to spring sinks first of all into such a sleep." — Ziegler

The first instance of *tardemah* in the Bible occurs in the Garden of Eden before the fall of man. God crafts a perfect environment for Adam and sets the stage for one of the most unusual stories in the creation account.

GOD WAS NOT ENOUGH

God walked with His man in the cool of the evening. He blessed man with everything, including a need that God "in person" would never be able to fulfill! It is interesting to note that God created Adam with an inborn need for fellowship and relationality which would never be satisfied by the divine presence alone! As strange as this may first appear, it is nonetheless the truth! Even in a perfect, unfallen condition, Adam was "in need."

CREATION WAS NOT ENOUGH

A perfect environment didn't erase the longings Adam felt. Naming all the creatures in God's world didn't satisfy his need.

Extending God's moral rule to the universe did not reduce Adam's hunger for what would make him complete! Adam, in all of his unfallen capacities, was able to discern the very nature of every creature and name them accordingly, yet the Scripture states:

"...but for Adam there was not found a helper suitable for him." (Gen. 2:20.)

The man God created could not identify that for which he longed! The grandeur of unfallen creation wasn't enough.

The animals weren't enough. *God wasn't enough.* All his efforts to identify, order and categorize the universe were not enough! Adam, after all his efforts, was left deeply unfulfilled, longing for something he could not find and did not understand. Adam became God's first candidate for a *tardemah.* It is at this point in Adam's story that God enters the scene with a timely gift:

"So the Lord God caused a deep sleep to fall upon the man, and he slept..."(Gen. 2:21).

Here is the first appearance of *tardemah* in the Bible! God encounters an obedient, sinless, yet incomplete Adam trapped in what I call the "darkness of unknowing." After all his best attempts at meeting his own needs, God graciously grants a "deep sleep" that will change his life forever.

ENTER THE *TARDEMAH* OF UNKNOWING

Notice the chief component in what we're calling the *Tardemah of Unknowing*:

NEEDINESS

One can walk in close fellowship with the Lord, using all one's gifts and abilities to name things correctly for others, while at the same time, possessing deep and abiding unmet needs.

Such needs and longings cannot be answered by any previous or present experience, status or attainment. It is a *Darkness of Unknowing,* for all you know is what you *don't* need!

IT IS NOT A SIN TO NEED

Adam's condition demonstrates to all of us that to "need," even to "need deeply," is not necessarily to "sin." Adam was not rebuked by God because God's *direct presence* wasn't enough. God created him that way! God even allowed Adam to live for a season with a felt sense of his unmet longings. Nothing he ate, drank or named afforded Adam any relief from his deepest hunger.

There are many types of human need. We will examine four here:

FOUR TYPES OF NEED

Proverbs 30:15,16 declares:

"...There are three things that will not be satisfied, four that will not say, 'enough:' sheol, and the barren womb, earth that is never satisfied with water, and fire that never says, "enough'."

This interesting passage underscores *four kinds of need.* The word pictures are as remarkable as they are unforgettable.

- The insatiable hunger of the *grave.*
- The insatiable longing of the *barren womb.*
- The insatiable thirst of the *dry earth.*
- The insatiable need of *fire.*

The literal Hebrew says that none of the above ever cry, "wealth or enough!" They are: *The Grave – Needs Met Only in the World to Come*

Some needs heaven alone will satisfy. The grave is just such an example. For the *grave* to be satisfied and to cease crying for *more*, we will have to wait for the *world to come.* Such a hope will be realized only at the end of the Age when God, Himself, reverses the curse of death. The *grave* speaks to us of those needs which can never be fully satisfied in this life. There are certain needs only heaven can fulfill. God has made it that way. To expect such needs to be met on earth would be to doom oneself to a life of unbearable frustration and despair.

C.S. Lewis once said:

"If I find in myself a desire which no experience in this world can satisfy, the most probable explanation is that I was made for another world."

The Barren Womb – Needs Met by Single Instances of Grace

Some needs require only one answer. The *barren womb* represents just such longings. In the case of the *barren womb*, a child would be a full and complete answer. Think of the last time God brought one complete answer in response to a prayer. What you experienced was a *single instance of grace!*

The Dry Earth – *Needs Met Only by a Continual Outpouring of Specific Provision*

Some needs are so deep that they require an inundation of blessings. The *dry earth* speaks to us of needs which can also be met, yet which require more than single instances of grace. Like thirsty ground, some needs require an inundation over extended periods of time. If we confuse these types of need with those met by single instances of grace, great confusion and frustration will be the result.

Fire – *Needs That Are Met Only Through Abstinence*

Some needs can only be met by not engaging them at all. The imagery of *fire* is unique in all of the above types of need. Fire singes all that comes near it, consuming all combustibles in its path. Fire I take to be the universal symbol of *lust*: the fire, which is never put out but is only enlarged through indulgence. The fires of lust, in any form, can only be conquered by never engaging them to begin with, i.e. total abstinence!

For instance, the heroin addict with ten years sobriety can never again be a "recreational" heroin user. To touch such a powerful drug would be to feed the flames of lust all over again! The only way to beat such an opponent is to never get into the ring with him at all.

- Is your present need able to be met only in the world to come? If so, then this is a *grave need.*
- Can your present need be met by a single instance of Grace? If so, then this is a *barren womb need.*
- Does your current need require an inundation of many instances of grace? If so, then yours is a *dry earth need.*
- Is your most current longing demanding some form of addictive indulgence, if so this is a *fire need.*

ARE YOU IN NEED OF A *TARDEMAH* OF UNKNOWING?

Are you:

- Walking with God as faithfully as you can?
- Doing much to further His work and, in the process, naming so many things for others around you?
- Free from flagrant overt sin, yet a sense of incompleteness keeps gnawing at the core of your being?
- Unable to fully identify or properly meet your need?
- Is even Eden becoming a distasteful place?

If so, then you need to sleep! You need a divine *tardemah*. You need the type of surgery God will soon pour out in abundance. It equals an operation wherein God reaches in and turns your deepest longings into reality.

ADAM'S WAY OF NEGATION

To get to what it is that you do *need,* you must often first identify what you *don't need.* This is called the *way of negation.* The *way of negation* is simply stating what something is *not.* For instance, teenagers often say, "I'm not my dad;" "I'm not my mom;" "I don't like this;" "I don't like that;" but they are not quite sure what they "like," or "who" they are. So it was with Adam.

In naming creation, Adam was confronted with a steady stream of realities that were wonderful and good in and of themselves, but they in no way met his deepest need. All Adam knew was that everything he had seen and experienced wasn't *it*! I believe like Adam, you too will "know *it* when you see it," but God Himself must bring the answer to your need, an answer that comes only after He first puts you "to sleep" for surgery

"And the Lord God caused the deep sleep to fall upon Adam, and he slept; and he took one of his ribs, and closed up the flesh instead thereof:" (Gen. 2:21)

Notice that Adam's need was met only after a *divine sleep* anesthetized him in order for God to open him up for surgery. God took part of Adam, and with that part, He cre-

19

ated Eve. Adam went to sleep helpless, yet he woke up prepared to receive the greatest blessing of his life!

GOD DETERMINES, YOU DISCOVER

We can never initiate a sovereign *tardemah* visitation, any more than we could will to dream a dream while in a waking state. Yet we can make ourselves available and responsive to divine visitation.

If you are longing for something, that nothing you presently possess can satisfy, then you are a candidate for the *Tardemah of Unknowing.*

God has encoded many deep and complex longings into your creaturely DNA. He *determines* them; you *discover* them. *Deep calleth unto deep.*

The deep cry of your soul can only be answered by a corresponding depth in God. Just as thirst is good evidence that such a thing as water exists, and hunger is good evidence that food exists, so also your deepest unmet longing is a proof that God exists and possesses the only answer that will truly satisfy. Take heart. Soon He will come to you. You will sleep and then you will wake to find the God given answer to your deepest need.

"And the rib, which the Lord God had taken from man, made he a woman, and brought her unto the man. And Adam said, this is now bone of my bones, and flesh of my flesh…" (Gen. 2:22,23)

The *Tardemah of Unknowing* involves extensive surgery on the inner man after which God walks into our lives the particular answer we've been unable to discover in our own strength. As you prepare to pray for a *Tardemah of Unknowing*, it is important to realize that each *tardemah* should be studied, meditated upon, and then sought after much preparation of heart. Soak in each of the three truths the *tardemahs* reveal, knowing with confidence that God will meet you at the altar of a willing and prepared heart.

We will speak of this *tardemah* in its global application

in Chapter Five. I believe that the *tardemah of unknowing* in-volves the naming and meeting of *impossible needs*. Adam's longing could only be met by the creation of a "new thing" that had never existed before. It was therefore *impossible* for Adam to meet his own need. God had to do it! God will do the same for you!

QUESTIONS FOR REFLECTION

• Adam was allowed to live "in need" for an extended period of time. This served to awaken in him a hunger only God could fill. Are you currently hungering for something your present surroundings and abilities have been unable to satisfy?

• Adam could not, for all his seeking, find the answer to his deepest longing. This served to point him away from himself and toward God. Are you finding yourself more and more aware of the fact that only God can meet your deepest longings?

• Adam stood in need of something utterly new if his needs were to be met. Are you sensing that God has a blessing uniquely crafted for your situation? Be patient. Adam's "impossible need" was met, but only after he was reduced to a *sleep* of utter dependence and *trust*.

A PRAYER FOR A *TARDEMAH* OF UNKNOWING

Let's pray and ask God to intervene in our lives. Let's ask Him to do *something* impossible. Let's pray to receive a *Tardemah of Unknowing*.

"Heavenly Father, I acknowledge that you have created me in Your image. I accept that possessing deep neediness is not sinful. I confess my ignorance as to what will fulfill my deepest longings. I lay myself before You in a posture of vulnerability and utter dependence. I freely, without shame, or embarrassment, invite You to bring me the deep and profound surgery my soul requires. Please remove what hinders my freedom. Open my eyes to the truth I need to see. I give You access to all the rooms of my soul where hiddeness and secret wounds have controlled me. I surrender in hope, trusting that You will walk a full and complete deliverance into my life."

In Jesus' name.

CHAPTER THREE

The *Tardemah* of Divine Destiny

"Healings, deliverances, visions, courage, strength, and new insights often come to saints during the sleep process."
—Dick Mills

The previous chapter dealt with the *tardemah* that comes in answer to the deepest and often unknown needs of life. This chapter will deal with another specific need; one that is equally unmeetable in our own strength. It is the *tardemah* which comes as a "reconfirmation" of divine destiny.

Are you in need of a reconfirmation of the "life word" God has given you? Do you need a fresh impartation of God's power in order to fulfill your destiny? Don't feel bad, so did Abraham.

GOD PREPARES ANOTHER SLEEPING PILL

Genesis chapter fifteen portrays the great patriarch Abraham some ten years into his journey of faith. Abraham was the man God had chosen in order to create His covenant people in the earth. Abraham had been a pagan worshiper in a city called Ur. God called him to leave his native country and to go to a land God would afterward show him. Abraham obeyed and awaited the fulfillment of God's promise for his life.

God promised Abraham a son, yet his wife's barrenness, their shared old age, and every other life circumstance made the hope of fulfillment seem like fantasy. Abraham, like most of us, began to wonder if his future hopes would ever be realized. He stood in desperate need of a *reconfirmation* of his divine destiny.

A THREEFOLD ANATOMY OF PROMISE

There were three phases in Abraham's journey of faith. Together they equal a threefold *anatomy of promise.*

Throughout redemptive history God's promises follow a predictable pattern. Familiarity with this pattern will enable us to better understand where *we are* in our current faith experience.

- First, *the promise is given.*
- Second, *the promise is obscured.*
- Third, *the promise is fulfilled.*

We will examine all three of these stages in Abraham's life in order to gain a better understanding of both the timing and significance of his *Tardemah of Divine Destiny.*

PHASE 1: *THE PROMISE GIVEN*

"Life words" characteristically come in spectacular, if not grandiose packages. God encounters Abram while still in the blush of youthful invincibility. He is a bold man, a good man, a man willing to risk everything on a God-ordained adventure. Genesis 12:1-3 says,

"Now the Lord had said unto Abram, Get thee out of thy country, and from thy kindred, and from thy father's house, unto a land that I will show thee: and I will make of thee a great nation, and I will bless thee, and make thy name great; and thou shalt be a blessing... And in thee shall all families of the earth be blessed."

It is important to remember that God always plants the seeds of destiny in unplowed and immature soil. God's promise to Abram is as spectacular in its *interpretation* as it will be in its *application.*

"...he brought him forth abroad, and said, Look now toward heaven and tell the stars, if thou be able to number them: and he said unto him, so shall thy seed be." (Gen. 15:5)

God calls Abram out under the night sky and sets the entire universe before him! He then announces that Abram will become the progenitor of a *new race.* Abram is to be the *"living link"* between God and His *plan,* God and His *people,* and God and His *purposes.*

If ever there were an opportunity for *hubris* to enter a human heart, it would be here! Abram, however, embraces the "life word" with humility. ***"… He believed in the Lord; and he counted it to him for righteousness."*** (Gen. 15:6).

A PROMISE BIGGER THAN THE UNIVERSE

What is interesting about Abram's response to God is that far from feeling *dwarfed* before such a celestial display, Abram arguing from the "lesser to the greater," actually concludes from God's words that *he* is greater than the *stars in the heavens* and that *he* will receive blessings more numerous than all the *grains of sand* the world itself could contain! The *entire universe* will be but the backdrop against which Abram's important life of promise will be lived out! The universe is to be to him a mere *token - the token* of a promise far greater in scope and certainty. The *elements themselves* would one day "pass away," but *God's Word* will never pass away! Abram was now the "living link" between heaven and the very lineage which would one day produce the Savior of the world!

THE POWER OF PROPHETIC MEMORY

Why would God risk such a spectacular display of promise? The answer is simple. Abram needed something to *remember*! His future faith would depend upon the quality of his *memory!* It was necessary for Abram to believe that he and his descendants were superior to the "stars of the heavens" and the "sands of the sea". Why? Because *prophetic memory* alone can keep faith alive in difficult times.

Does Abraham's story sound familiar? Is the promise you've received bigger than you're comfortable speaking about? Does it sometimes seem that if all your streams of "promise" converge you'll be the next *Pope* or *whoever* represents greatness in your arena of calling? If so, then welcome to your generation.

I believe there are hundreds of millions of men, women, boys, and girls walking the earth today pregnant with incredible promise. Like Abraham, they bear within them the seeds of remarkable potential! They are *living, hoping, failing, learning, leading,* and many are simply *surviving.* I believe their season of fruitfulness is *just around the corner*! It would be *unnatural* for God to call any of His children to a place of true *Kingdom greatness* apart from impressing that reality *deeply* upon them.

When "life words" are given, they are intentionally spectacular. Impartations must be profound if "prophetic memory" is to fulfill its purpose. Abram's promise was *unforgettable.* It had to be; his future would depend upon it.

MEMORY AND HOPE

Memory is a valuable asset in our walk with God. Throughout scripture whenever "hope" is mentioned, it is usually found in tandem with an exercise of memory. Our very capacity to "hope" for anything is predicated upon our ability to "recall" an actual experience of divine intervention. *Memory* gives us a ground for *hope.* We *hope now* because we *remember "then."* We remember *"the days of old"* (Deuteronomy 32:7; Psalm 143:5). We remember *"His works"* (I Chronicles 16:12; Psalm 105:5). We remember *"His mercies"* (Ps. 25:7).

God's *past deliverances remembered* equal *hope!* The "stars" above Abram's head, the "sand" beneath his feet, the later circumcision of his flesh, all would serve as perpetual reminders "prodding" Abram daily to *memory* and *hope!* Eventually his "prophetic memory" would become so strong that the scriptures say of its exercise:

"...against hope (he) believed in hope that he might become the father of many nations according to that which was spoken, 'so shall thy seed be'". (Romans 4:18).

Abram's "memory" would be severely tested when a "twenty-year curtain" of barrenness descended upon him. It is at this point that his *Tardemah of Divine Destiny* was given.

ENTER A *TARDEMAH* OF DIVINE DESTINY

As we mentioned in Chapter One, the posture of sleep is one of vulnerability and submission wherein we relinquish all control to God. In the *Tardemah of Divine Destiny* we witness Abram's absolute powerlessness in the face of a humanly impossible destiny. As Abram wrestles with deep disappointment over his yet unrealized future, the Bible again reveals God approaching a frustrated servant with "divine sleep". The Scriptures declare:

"Now when the sun was going down, a deep sleep fell upon Abram..." (Gen. 15:12).

Tardemah! God is going to reconfirm His promise to Abram by restating his initial covenant oath. He will go even one step further than this by prophesying the *future* of Abram and his descendants:

"And God said to Abram, 'Know for certain that your descendants will be strangers in a land that is not theirs,'..." (Gen. 14:13).

Verse fourteen promises the ultimate judgment of Egypt and the subsequent wealth Abram's seed will inherit as they leave Egypt. He concludes in verse fifteen with a personal word of comfort:

"And as for you, you shall go to your fathers in peace; you shall be buried at a good old age."

God's voice of promise is heard yet again! Abram's destiny is secure! Yet God impresses an even deeper sense of security upon Abram's soul.

A STRANGE RITUAL WHILE ABRAM SLEEPS

What is also interesting about Genesis chapter fifteen is that verses nine and ten chronicle a strange request made to Abram by God:

"'...Bring me a three year old heifer, and a three year old female goat, and a three year old ram, and a turtle dove, and a young pigeon.' Then he brought all these to Him and cut them in two, and laid each half opposite the other..."

God required a *sacrifice* before fully *reconfirming* Abram's divine call. The Scriptures explain why in the following words:

"And it came about when the sun had set, that it was very dark, and behold, there appeared a smoking oven and

a flaming torch which passed between these pieces. On that day the Lord made a covenant with Abram ..." (Gen. 15: 17,18).

The glorious *reconfirmation* Abram sought occurred while he slept!

COVENANT SECURITY

The ritual describing God's presence as fire passing between the pieces of the sacrifice may seem strange to us today, but the imagery is pregnant with spiritual significance. In ancient times, two parties could enter into a *covenant relationship* by exchanging garments, weapons, a sacrifice and a sacred meal. By sworn oath, two individuals, tribes, or peoples could become one in *covenant commitment*. The shedding of "covenant blood" bound individuals or peoples into an inviolable union perpetual to all their generations. The covenant sacrifice would be laid out in pieces as its representatives walked through the pieces swearing to uphold the covenant oath (Jer. 34:18). Marriage is the only vestige in our culture of this once powerful "covenant ceremony" that bound peoples and tribes together from time immemorial.

TWO TYPES OF COVENANT

There were essentially two types of covenant: the *conditional* and the *unconditional*. In a *conditional* covenant, as long as one met his or her side of the bargain, their covenant obligation was complete. If it were violated, horrible consequences would ensue. In an *unconditional* covenant, however, one party and one party alone, swore covenant allegiance, protection, and perpetual provision, regardless of the imperfection of the other party. The portrait of "deep sleep" falling upon Abram is significant in that it equals a *tardemah* visitation wherein God personally lays His covenant partner down, puts him to sleep, then takes the "covenant walk" through the pieces of the sacrifice *alone*, unilaterally promising complete faithfulness in maintaining and fulfilling Abram's destiny!

Abram received *absolute assurance* of his future *as he slept*! The reconfirmation he had been longing for finally came. It was a one-sided, unconditional guarantee of promise and destiny!

WHAT ABOUT ME GOD?

You are also called by God! Christ, your covenant Lord, has died in your place. He has fulfilled every condition for your absolute acceptance! Have time and circumstance conspired to threaten your hopes with impossibility? Do common sense and wisdom alike seem to militate against the idea of your "impossible dream"? Have you cried out in frustration for the very fruitfulness God has promised you? Don't despair, He will answer you, but first He may have to visit you with a season of "divine sleep".

Abram awoke re-encouraged, certain that he was on the right path. God Himself would fulfill His "impossible dream." God alone was to be the *author* and *finisher* of Abram's destiny. The same is true for you! God has spoken to you in the past, yet setbacks have wearied you. Don't be discouraged; remember Paul's encouraging words to Timothy:

"This command I entrust to you, Timothy, my son, in accordance with the prophecies previously made concerning you, that by them you may fight the good fight." (I Tim. 1:18)

Fight against despair; *war* using the prophecies you have received as weapons against hopelessness. "Wait upon the Lord", and He will reconfirm your destiny. In the *Tardemah of Unknowing*, we discover a God who reveals and then fulfills our deepest longings. In the *Tardemah of Divine Destiny* we witness a condition of absolute powerlessness which then gives way to God's unlimited resources of hope and certainty. Always remember God has *determined* your destiny. You merely *discover* it. God sees your *future* and *past* in one simultaneous *now*. He is powerful enough to make:

"All things work together for good to them that love God, to them who are the called according to his purpose," (Rom. 8:28).

Just as a freeway *sign* is not the *destination* itself, but merely a reconfirmation that you are still going in the right direction, so also God will give you *signs* that will reconfirm the visions and purposes He has placed within you. If many years have gone by yet barrenness persists, if the sand of wilderness years has temporarily clouded your vision of the future, hold on! For as surely as you are wide awake right now, God has an appropriate visitation of "divine sleep" to restore your hope and fulfill your destiny!

PHASE II — THE PROMISE OBSCURED

Well after Abraham's *tardemah* experience he entered the second phase of his life of faith, a time when extraordinary promise would give way to a prolonged season of personal *fruitlessness*. "Twenty years" of barrenness threatened to *obscure* the promises of God. A vision larger than the universe itself would now fall into the ground and die. Even more shocking, it was to die at Abraham's own hand!

Did you know that before "life words" can be truly implemented, we must *intentionally* or *unintentionally* destroy any possibility of their human fulfillment?

Even Abraham's *name,* which meant *exalted father,* would become a point of embarrassment during his years of trial. Every mention of if would point him either to the "fact" of "God's promise" or to the "twin reality" of his utter "barrenness." Thank God for the "memory" of Abraham's *Tardemah of Divine Destiny*!

William D. Mounce notes:

> "God used barren wives to show that His continued blessing of the world came not through human, but through His divine means. Jesus came from a nation descended from barren wombs. Only through God's direct intervention would that nation and our Savior have existed."

THE SON OF LAUGHTER

"And the Lord visited Sarah as he had said, ... for Sarah conceived, and bare Abraham a son in his old age,

...and Abraham called the name of his son that was born unto him, whom Sarah bare to him, Isaac... and Abraham was an hundred years old, when his son Isaac was born unto him." (Gen. 21:1-5)

The "twenty-year curtain" obscuring Abraham's promise was lifted only at the birth of Isaac. Abraham would have twelve years of bliss watching Isaac grow up before him. His every hope was fulfilled. Faith had given way to sight! With Isaac present there was no further need for Abraham to exercise faith as he had in the past. Isaac would now become God's "living link" in the earth, the "linch pin" holding the very hinges of the door of redemption securely in place!

Just imagine it. Each day Isaac lived and grew, God's people moved one step closer to the birth of their Messiah. While God alone is the *efficient cause* or *source* of redemption, Isaac in his lifetime was the *instrumental cause* - the very vehicle *through which* redemption would come to mankind. Think of it! A safer child could not be found anywhere on earth! In his time, Isaac was the most important young man on the planet. The child of promise always is!

Wouldn't you sleep well at night if you knew premature death was an impossibility? Wouldn't your life be one of peace and rest if you knew that all the powers of hell let loose couldn't harm a single hair on your head? For a time, "salvation history" was bound up entirely in the life of *one child*! One knife thrust to Isaac would have assassinated God's dream for mankind! One mortal blow to this "Son of Laughter" and the coming of Jesus Christ would have been severely hindered, if not stopped altogether! No demonic hand could harm Isaac, *but Abraham's could*, and now at God's command it *must!*

PHASE III: THE PROMISE FULFILLED

It may sound initially strange, but it is at the point of Abraham's greatest personal sacrifice that his deepest personal fulfillment will be realized.

- The Promise was given.
- The Promise was obscured for a time.
- The Promise will now be fulfilled on God's terms.

God fulfills our "life words" only at the point of our complete and unconditional surrender. Every vision God gives must die. We must never forget that God is more interested in our *character* than He is our *comfort*. He is more concerned that we *be good* than that we *feel good*. And in the final analysis God will frequently *hurt us*, but He will never *harm us*.

Abraham will now experience a spiritual "mid-life crisis" and a corresponding "paradigm shift" that will raise him to a new level of faith and intimacy with God.

THE PARADOX OF PROMISE

Abraham, after walking twelve years in his promised inheritance through Isaac, is now given a command that seems to fly in the face of reason itself!

"Take now thy son, thine only son Isaac, whom thou lovest, and get thee into the Land of Moriah; and offer him there for a burnt offering upon one of the mountains which I will tell thee of." (Gen. 22:2)

Wait a minute! This doesn't sound right! How could this be God! How can you kill what can't be killed? How could it ever be in God's best interest to destroy His own plan! How will *world redemption* ever be realized if Isaac is sacrificed?

Can you feel the tension building? Can you sense even a little confusion in Abraham's heart? He is to take Isaac who *cannot die* and *kill him*? Even worse, he is to offer him as a *burnt offering*. This meant that he would have to *kill* Isaac, after which his remains would be reduced to ashes. *God's Promise reduced to ashes? Impossible!*

Abraham, at God's express command will now take what *cannot die* apart from fulfillment and *reduce it to ashes*. Are we willing to allow our *Isaacs* to be reduced to ashes? The Scriptures declare,

"By faith Abraham, when he was tried, offered up Isaac; and he that had received the promises offered up

his only begotten son, of whom it was said, that in Isaac shall Thy seed be called; accounting that God was able to raise Him up, even from the dead;…" (Heb. 11:17-19)

You may have "heard" this story a million times before. I only hope you can "feel it" now! Only at the point of sacrifice does Abraham's life takes a decided turn toward greatness!

"Abraham rose up early in the morning, and saddled his ass and took two of his young men with him, and Isaac his son, and clave the wood for the burnt offering, and rose up, and went unto the place of which God had told him…." (Gen. 22:3).

THE FIRE AND THE KNIFE

"In principle," I understand the dynamics of the story. "Give freely back to God what He has given you, etc." But "in practice," as a father myself, this seems almost inconceivable to me! To take my son, Grant, with all our shared love and life together; to watch his face, tears of fear welling up in his eyes while I lay him down on a wood-laden altar; to then *kill* him with a knife and then *reduce him to ashes*! I don't know if I could do it. Yet the Bible says:

"… Abraham took the wood of the burnt offering, and laid it upon Isaac, his son, and he took the fire in his hand and a knife and they went both of them together. And Isaac spake unto Abraham his father, and said, my father: And he said here am I, my son. And he said behold the fire and the wood; but where is the lamb for a burnt offering? And Abraham said, my son, God will provide Himself a lamb for a burnt offering; so they went both of them together. And they came to the place which God had told him of; and Abraham built an altar there, and laid the wood in order, and bound Isaac his son, and laid him upon the altar upon the wood. And Abraham stretched forth his hand to slay his son." (Gen. 22:6-7, 9-10)

What on earth is going on? What is God up to? How could such a command contribute in any way to the fulfillment of God's promises? *I'll let you in on the secret!* I believe God's intention in this command was to *win Abraham back!* "Back from what?" you ask. Back from years of being *consumed by* "an abstract promise". Abraham had lived for years *believing* and *hoping* in "promises" of personal blessing which would be realized always in some *future event, experience,* or *far off occurrence.* With Isaac's death now a foregone conclusion in Abraham's mind, we notice that his focus shifts drastically *away from* the "means" (Isaac) and *back to* the "source" (God). From the "blessing" Abraham will now turn to the "Blessor," instead of the "promise" he will now embrace the "Promise Giver," from "provision" alone he will turn to the "Provider." Even at the risk of the *world's salvation,* Abraham is willing to obey.

Nothing makes sense anymore. Abraham enters "mid-life" free of youthful certainties. He didn't even question the morality of the command. Who could? Life belongs to God. He can therefore demand what is His any time and in any way He chooses.

THE SACRIFICE ON MOUNT MORIAH

"And Abraham stretched forth his hand, and took the knife to slay his son… And the angel of the Lord called unto him out of heaven, and said, … Lay not thine hand upon the lad, neither do thou any thing unto him…" (Gen. 22:10, 11-12)

At this point, we must ponder some weighty questions:
* Whose life was really offered on the mountain?
* Was Isaac even the main character in the story?
* Was the sacrificial knife stayed that day?

With the answers to these questions, we will arrive at the "true fulfillment" of Abraham's "life word". The answers are illuminating. It was *Abraham* being sacrificed that day, not Isaac. *Abraham's will* was what God was after. The sacrificial knife was *not* stayed that day, for a complete and acceptable sacrifice was offered to God – *Abraham himself!* Two thousand years later, Jesus Christ would mirror a similar and absolute surrender and on the *very ground* where

Abraham had raised his knife! This ground of "uncondi-tional surrender" would one day support the very *cross of Jesus Christ!*

Abraham walks down from the mountain having entered *middle age,* a *new ministry,* and a *new found sense of inti-macy with God.* Anything that stands between us and God must go. Nothing now stood between God and Abraham, *not even God's promise*! Nothing else mattered anymore. Isaac or no Isaac, promise or no promise, Abraham has exchanged them all for *God Himself!*

Abraham's search has come full circle. His journey *began* with God. It will now *end* in God. God seems willing to destroy any promise if that's what it takes for our focus to return exclusively to Him. Like Abraham, we must decide if we are willing to give up *God's promise* for *God's face!* Abraham's *Tardemah of Divine Destiny,* given in Genesis chapter fifteen, provided the *covenant bond* which held Abraham securely in hope even through his disastrous trip to Egypt, the birth of Ishmael, and now the offering of his son.

QUESTIONS FOR REFLECTION:

• Abraham held a unique place in the redemptive econ-omy of God. Do you ever feel that you are destined to ful-fill a great task for God's kingdom? If so, what is it?

• Abraham experienced a prolonged "season of barren-ness" on the heels of promise. Have you ever endured a "season of fruitlessness" that seemed the polar opposite of what God had promised you?

• Abraham was a humble man at every point in his life. Are you humble in your calling, or do you secretly believe yourself to be "superior to" or more "anointed than" others?

• Abraham created *Ishmael* in a fleshly attempt to "help God" fulfill his purpose. Are you currently using some "fleshly means" in order to manipulate or hasten the perfor-mance of your promise?

A PRAYER FOR A *TARDEMAH* OF DIVINE DESTINY

Let's lay our "destinies" upon God's altar and pray again that *His* will would be done in our lives.

"Heavenly Father, I lay before You all my expectations concerning the future. Cleanse me from all fantasies of my own making. Burn away the wood, hay, and stubble of my own projections Purify the gold and silver of my true prophetic promise. Heal any remaining wounds of disappointment and disillusionment due to hopes that have been deferred. I acknowledge that I cannot control Your sovereign will. I simply surrender to it. Forgive my transgressions and pour Your favor upon me. Please reconfirm the destiny You have designed for me."

In Jesus' name.

CHAPTER FOUR

The Tardemah of Utter Grace

"Such is our path, and such the grace of God, that our falls and mistakes may be a means to nurture our true growth; as a tree extracts fresh strength from the soil which is enriched by its own decaying leaves and fallen blossoms." —Andrew Jukes

Our first two *tardemah*s dealt essentially with two good men; men met by God in the midst of divine favor and blessing. Adam was enjoying unbroken fellowship with God. Abraham was enjoying prosperity and was yet to birth his Ishmael. We can all understand why God would honor obedient and exemplary servants, but what about a *tardemah* for those with a shameful past?

WHAT IS PAST IS PROLOGUE

In Jacob's story, we encounter a *Tardemah of Utter Grace;* a grace so all encompassing that it redeems wasted years and replaces devoured harvests. Adam's *Tardemah of Unknowing* answers to our need for inner transformation. Abraham's *Tardemah of Divine Destiny* addresses God's willingness to reconfirm the "life words" He has given. Jacob's "deep sleep" and subsequent dream life will offer hope to all those who have a past desperately in need of redemption

JACOB THE YO-YO

Jacob was a yo-yo. We've all seen yo-yos; they go up and down and up and down, hypnotizing with their motion. Such was Jacob's life. It swung from the dizzying heights of divine revelation to the crushing depths of moral failure, from the pinnacle of holiness to the dregs of despair. There is very little "middle ground" in Jacob's history.

JACOB THE HEEL CATCHER

Jacob, the second son of Isaac and Rebekah and twin brother of Esau, was a spoiled, selfish, and deceitful brat! He cheated and lied his way into every conceivable difficulty. His very name, *Yaaqob*, testified to his nature. The name meant "heel catcher," "trickster," or "supplanter." Unfortunately, the name proved an adequate description of the man. Theologian, Herbert Lockyer, called Jacob, "the Doctor Jekyll and Mr. Hyde of the Bible", yet he would die at 147 years of age a blessed and happy man, having fulfilled the will of God for his generation! How can this be? Simply because: God is gracious!

THE RESUME OF A PATRIARCHAL LEADER

Let's categorize the kinds of "badness" we're talking about so that we might grasp the depth of grace God extends to this unique servant. Try to imagine a *resume* listing Jacob's qualifications for a patriarchal leadership position:

Weaknesses:
- Steals birthrights. (Gen. 25:29-34)
- Deceives authority figures.(Gen. 27:1-29,41)
- Runs away and never faces or resolves conflict situations. (Gen. 28:1-5)
- His deceitfulness backfires on him creating unimaginable domestic squabbles, from the deception of relatives to the anger and jealousy of multiple wives and concubines. (Gen. 29:15-30, 31-43)
- Loss and tragedy seem to follow his dysfunctional family and any one choosing to associate with them:
- His daughter is violated. (Gen. 34:1-5)
- His sons Simeon and Levi murderously avenge her at great personal cost to Jacob's reputation. (Gen. 34:1-31)
- Deborah, a beloved family nurse and friend, dies. (Gen. 35:16)
- Rachel, the love of his life, dies. (Gen. 35:16)

- His son Reuben defiles his concubine, Bilhah. (Gen. 35:22)
- Joseph, the joy of Jacob's life, is lost for years and presumed dead. (Gen. 37:34)
- In his old age, Jacob has to flee from his home in the midst of famine for a new life in Egypt. (Gen. 46:3)

Strengths:
- Jacob had a vision and made vows to God (Gen. 28:20-22), but only after twenty-eight years of procrastination did he fulfill them. (Gen. 35:1-15)
- He made it back to the Promised Land (Gen. 31-32) (He occasionally arrived on time).
- He met God in a new way, received a new name, and reconciled with his brother. (Gen. 32-33) (Unfortunately his past sins had to drive him there in utter desperation).

Do your qualifications for ministry match up to these?

Jacob was a thief, a liar, a deceptive son, a selfish brother, a bad husband, and a lenient father, BUT HE WAS ALSO GOD'S MAN!

ABRAHAM, ISAAC, AND ???

The Bible is replete with references to "The God of Abraham, Isaac and ???" *Why **Jacob**, of course!* It's hard to imagine any other name in this patriarchal list, but it is doubtful that Jacob ever thought himself worthy of a place in the patriarchal "hall of fame"! A brief overview of his family of origin will go a long way toward helping us understand the nature of his transgressions and his corresponding need for a *Tardemah of Utter Grace.*

A HOUSE DIVIDED

Jacob's parents had a divided marriage, which in turn produced a divided family, occasioning a division in Jacob's soul only God Himself could heal. Jacob's parents each had a *favorite child.* Isaac chose *Esau*, "rugged man of the world." Rebekah chose *Jacob*, a "smooth man," the opposite of his brother in every way. Undue favoritism tore Jacob's family apart.

THE ROOTS OF FAVORITISM

Isaac failed as a father in his favoritism of Esau over Jacob. Rebekah failed as a mother by rejecting Esau and smothering Jacob. The division in the marriage created a breech between child and parent. Jacob couldn't help but resent Isaac for choosing Esau. Esau most certainly resented his mother's plots and schemes against him. Finally, even Jacob and Esau were at odds with one another. Jacob, later in life, would continue this generational family trait when favoritism for his youngest son Joseph would provoke a murderous rage in his other children.

THE FRUITS OF FAVORITISM

The tree of favoritism yields only two kinds of fruit, both bitter. In one, it encourages "over confidence;" *Esau's attitude*. In another, it promotes "deep insecurity;" *Jacob's attitude*. Favoritism contributed to an insecurity in Jacob which soon grew into a threefold curse of *mistrust, fear, and deception.*

JACOB S THREEFOLD CURSE
Jacob and Trust

Isaac's favoritism for Esau produced a deep insecurity in Jacob's heart. Jacob didn't trust his father to hear from God nor his brother to yield the birthright even at God's direction. After awhile, he couldn't even trust the wisdom or motives of his mother. *Trust issues* were at the top of Jacob's *recovery list*.

Jacob and Fear

Next came *issues of fear*. Not only had undue favoritism bequeathed its legacy of *inferiority* and *mistrust*, but the *facts* of Jacob's life didn't seem to encourage any hope of the promise of the birthright. Jacob and his mother believed

Esau to be unworthy of the birthright. They feared that Isaac, now old and set in his ways, would never give this legacy to Jacob. Fears were mounting! Everyone loved Esau, "a hairy man," a "man's man," yet most importantly, Isaac loved him and "did eat of his venison." Surely the dim-eyed old man would yield to his fleshly favoritism and frustrate God's plan for Jacob's life! Add to this, mother's scheming, which further fueled Jacob's insecurities, and you've got one big mess! Rebekah didn't trust Isaac. She didn't trust Esau. Neither she nor Jacob trusted God!

Once God becomes the object of mistrust, we are thrown all the more back upon ourselves. Isolation soon becomes the unholy breeding ground for fear in all of its forms. Jacob would say later in life: *"All these things be against me."* Well, very early in life, everything *did* seem to be against him! His greatest fears seemed justified.

GAZING OR GLANCING; THE PROBLEM OF FOCUS

Adding further to the already complicated circumstances of Jacob's life, was the fact that he and his mother had lost a *felt-sense* of God's presence. They couldn't have acted the way they did without this being the case. Once we move away from intimate union with the *Promise Giver*, in time, even His greatest *promises* seem surreal. How is it that Jacob could so easily doubt the clearest of divine promises? Usually the answer is found in one word: *focus!* When I *gaze* at God and merely *glance* at my circumstances, I tend to rise above all roadblocks to my destiny; however, if I *gaze* at the storms of life and merely *glance* at God, I soon loose sight of the clearest of His promises. Like a branch removed from its source of life, we too can become dry and spiritually brittle simply because we haven't experienced God's presence in a while. As Jacob's closeness to the *Promise Giver* became a dim memory, so the fulfillment of God's *promises* seemed more and more something Jacob had to control!

Jacob and Deception

Favoritism contributed to the *insecurity*, which flowered into *mistrust*; circumstances seemed to confirm Jacob's greatest *fears*. Now, *fear* will give birth to one of its ugliest offspring: *deception*. Once we project our *mistrust* onto the heavens, *fear* more than justifies any number of actions we would normally consider morally repugnant. When *fear* consumes *hope*, human beings become capable of almost anything! Jacob and Rebekah, now distanced from a felt-sense of God's presence, justify their deception of both Isaac and Esau, as being an appropriate *means* to a spiritual *end.* Here then, are the three unhealed *life issues* that would prove Jacob's undoing: *trust, fear, and deception.*

JACOB WAS RESPONSIBLE

The explanation of these three primary roots, however, in no way removes responsibility from Jacob. *Responsibility implies the ability to respond!* Jacob was, as we are, fully responsible for his every life decision! While we could not control the initial woundings we received in life, we are nonetheless responsible for every personal decision we have made thereafter. Jacob was guilty! We are guilty! All the kindling in the world piled in a heap will never *cause* a fire. Fire alone *causes* a fire. Jacob's family of origin *contributed* to Jacob's past for sure, but they didn't *cause* his sin. Jacob did! Lack of *trust* and persistent *fear* led to covert acts of *deception* deliberately designed to seize control of situations which were never Jacob's responsibility to begin with.

A FAMILIAR PATTERN

Does this pattern sound familiar? Is it hard for you to trust anyone, including God? Is it doubly hard to believe stupendous promises, when all the *facts* around you point only to doubt and fear? Have you ever tried to *help God out* in the meeting of your needs by *taking over* in your own strength?

Jacob's story sounds so familiar because Jacob's past is the pattern of our lives! *Mistrust, fear* and *deception* are at the root of all human frailty.

HITTING, LEAVING, OR DEMEANING

When you failed, were you *punished* or *threatened with punishment?* Were you *abandoned or threatened with the withdrawal of love?* Were you *demeaned, treated as though you had no value*? Did you know that God never uses these methods when redemptively correcting His children?

He never says, *"That's enough, you're going to hell,"* (hitting) or, *"That's it, you're never going to see Me again,"* (leaving) or, *"You worthless scum, you'll never amount to anything"* (demeaning). God doesn't employ *punishment, abandonment,* or *demeaning* with His children, because such non-relational methods only reinforce a "fear of punishment", a "fear of abandonment", and a corresponding sense of "worthlessness"! They may produce short-term behavioral changes, but never lasting results. God never uses such methods because they never end in true repentance. *Trust issues* can never be healed by threats of punishment. *Fear issues* are never assuaged by the withdrawal of love, and *deception* is never satisfactorily addressed through tirades or damning epitaphs. *We* may *punish, reject,* or *demean* in an attempt to control or modify the behavior of others, but *God does not*! How then does God redeem a past like Jacob's? The answer is the same in every age: by His grace!

BETHEL AND PENIEL — TWO STAGES IN JACOB S LIFE

There were two steps in God's strategy for the redemption of Jacob's past. They are marked by two vastly different *God encounters.* One occurs at *Bethel* (Gen. 28:10-22), the other at *Peniel* (Gen. 32:24-32). In the first encounter Jacob unwittingly enters *The House of God.* In the second, he will behold the very *Face of God*! The *Tardemah of Utter Grace* experienced at *Bethel* will serve as the forerunner to Jacob's "name changing" experience at *Peniel.* Even before Jacob was born, it was clearly prophesied that *he,* and not *Esau,* would inherit the birthright. Jacob's mother was told:

"...two nations are in the womb, and two manner of people shall be separated from thy bowels; and the one people shall be stronger than the other people; and the elder shall serve the younger." (Gen. 25:23)

This was a clear promise that Jacob would inherit the blessing of the firstborn. God sovereignly charged Jacob with the sacred responsibility of perpetuating the Messianic line! *Christ Himself* would one day come from Jacob's lineage!

THE GREAT ADDRESS

There is a clear "prophetic address" laid out in Scripture which, if followed, leads only to Jesus Christ. Messiah was to come from the *seed of Abraham* (Gen. 12:2,3; 22:18) He was to be a *son of Isaac* (Gen. 21:12) and most importantly he would be a *son of Jacob* (Num. 24:17). The Promise extended beyond Jacob to the *tribe of* his son *Judah* (Gen. 49:10). Finally to the *family of Jesse,* (Is. 11:1), the *house of David* (II Sam. 7:12-16; Jer. 23:5), Ending in an arrival at *Bethlehem* (Mic. 5:2) sometime before the destruction of Herod's Temple in 70 A.D. (Mal. 3:1; Ps. 118:26; Dan.9:26; Zech. 11:13; Hag. 2:7-9). One would assume that such a "heritage of promise" would have evoked a deep sense of hope and security in Jacob. It did not. From the womb, his life was marked by constant "unrest."

"Rebekah his wife conceived and the children struggled together within her." (Gen. 25:22).

"He took his brother by the heel in the womb..." (Hos. 12:3)

From wrestling to walking, to running, then wrestling again Jacob's was a see-saw existence.

ENTER A TARDEMAH OF UTTER GRACE: JACOB AT BETHEL/PERCEIVING THE HOUSE OF GOD

We should notice that God waits until Jacob is utterly unworthy of grace before he grants it. Jacob by now had lost any sense of his own personal *integrity* and *credibility*. In contemporary ministry terms, Jacob was a "fallen leader," certainly disqualified from pastoral or patriarchal leadership! He had broken faith with his father and brother through repeated acts of *deception*. Morally he was a life long and unrepentant *adulterer*, having adopted the pagan, yet biblically forbidden practice of multiple marriages! (A situation the Bible *describes*, but never *prescribes*.)

His deceit brought with it a stigma of mistrust that hung like a mist, poisoning every aspect of his life and ministry. For all intents and purposes, Jacob was worthy only of an *across the board condemnation*! Yet it is *here,* while desperately trying to outrun his past, that Jacob will "*happen upon the Holy."*

HAPPENING UPON THE HOLY

"And Jacob came out from Beersheba, and went toward Haran and he lighted upon a certain place, and tarried there all night ... and he dreamed." (Gen. 28:10-12)

Tardemah! Jacob will now finally encounter *the "deep sleep" that will awaken his dreams!* There is no such thing as "chance," "luck," or "coincidence" in God's Kingdom. Yet here the Bible seems to use the "language of chance":

"And he lighted upon a certain place..." (Gen. 28:11,)

Did Jacob simply "happen upon the Holy?" Of course not. Although personal sin had brought Jacob to this moment, it was God who superintended every step along the way. *"Oh Lord, I know that the way of man is not in himself; it is not in man that walketh to direct his steps."* (Jer. 10:23) God uses many *means* to accomplish His redemptive *ends.*

"... and he lighted upon a certain place ..."

At the end of Jacob's "spiritual rope," he "happens upon" *sacred ground.* I'm sure Jacob's enemies were hoping he would have "happened upon" a place of *judgment,* not the very *Gate of Heaven!* (Gen. 28:17). A simple rock from these severe surroundings would now be set up as an anointed pillar marking the place of divine visitation:

"Surely the Lord is in his place and I did not know it...and Jacob rose up early in the morning, and took the stone that he had put for his pillows, and set it up for a pillar, and poured oil upon the top of it. And he called the name of that place Bethel." (Genesis 28:16,18-19).

Jacob wakes after this profound *tardemah* visitation, yet his *leg* and *thigh* are still intact He is a yet *unbroken man.* God frequently grants His most profound visitations to children who are as of yet "unusable"!

He shows Jacob the *future,* yet it isn't time to touch him personally at the point of his greatest sin. This will require a "wrestling match" four chapters later.

Notice Jacob's initial reaction to his *Tardemah of Utter Grace:*

"and he was afraid...." (Gen. 28:17)

All Jacob concludes at this point in his life is that Bethel is an *"awesome place",* (Gen. 28:17), yet the chain of events that will lead to his ultimate "God encounter" begin here.

Notice *four things* about Jacob's *Tardemah of Utter Grace.* First, it was *unsought.* Second, it was *unexpected.* Third it was *unannounced.* Forth, it was *undeserved!* God is beginning to close in on Jacob. In fact, He's moving in for the kill. Soon Jacob will *die,* and Israel will be *born.*

It is important to notice that God is never "light on sin," but He does have a "light on sin." we do not possess! God sees the entire "boxtop" of the complicated puzzle of your life. He, alone, knows how to shape all the *chipped* and *ugly* pieces of your life into an overall "mosaic" of *meaning* and *purpose.* Only God can truly judge you!

This story isn't so much about *Jacob and his sin* as it is

about *God and His mercy*. Jacob leaves *Bethel* with some of his greatest sins and difficulties yet before him.

Genesis chapters 29 – 32 record "twenty years" of unimaginable *conflict*, *chastening*, and *confusion*. Yet the passing of so many years will leave Jacob still unresolved with regard to the *chief sin* of his life – the *deception* and *defrauding* of his brother.

> *Oh! God of Bethel, by whose hand*
> *Thy people still are fed,*
> *Who, through this weary pilgrimage*
> *Hast all our fathers led.*
> *Oh! spread Thy covering wings around*
> *'Til all our wanderings cease,*
> *And at our Father's loved abode*
> *Our souls arrive in peace.*

PENIEL: PERCEIVING THE FACE OF GOD

The redemption of Jacob's past began with his *tardemah* at Bethel. The final work however will be completed at *Peniel*!

"And he rose up that night, and took his two wives and his two women servants, and his eleven sons and passed over the ford Jabbok." (Gen. 32:22)

It is some "twenty years" since Jacob deceived his brother. Yet just as he is preparing to enter the Promised Land, who should appear again but *Esau*! Undealt with "Esaus" will always block our entrance into the Promise Land!

Jacob the *manipulator*, Jacob the *deceiver*, Jacob the *fixer*, true to character will now try to gain entrance to the Land by manipulating Esau yet again! By sending gifts to appease Esau's wrath, Jacob tries once more to *"manage"* the situation. But *Jacob* will never enter the Land of Promise; only *Israel* will. If God had allowed Jacob to take the Land via *deception* and *manipulation*, then God would have forfeited His own privilege of "giving the land" as a gift to Jacob and his descendents!

God must grab Jacob and stop him from entering the

TARDEMAH *The Deep Sleep That Awakens Your Dreams*

promise *illicitly*. In the middle of the night as Jacob contemplates his meeting with Esau, someone comes up from behind and grabs him!

A. B. Simpson says:

"It was night again... but it was different from the vision at Bethel. The danger was nearer now, and God was nearer, too. Then it was God at the 'top of the ladder', now God was 'on the level of Jacob', wrestling with him, having put Jacob in His very arms. Jacob was able to put his arms around his very God. God came very close to Jacob, because God wanted Jacob henceforth to live very near to Him."

WHAT IS YOUR NAME?

"So Jacob was left alone, and a man wrestled with him till daybreak. ... And he said unto him, what is thy name..." (Gen. 32:24, 27)

As Jacob *wrestles* with the strange night visitor, his entire life passes before his eyes.

The mirror-like waters of Jabbok reflect back a complex tapestry of lies and treachery. *"What is your name?"* the stranger asks. This is the same question his father Isaac had asked years before, as Jacob stood before him in an "Esau suit", *"Who is it?"*, Isaac asked. *"I am Esau, your first-born,"* Jacob replied. *"Are you really my son Esau?"*, he asked. *"I am,"* Jacob answered. (Gen. 26: 18 - 24)

With this *one deception*, the door was thrown open to a lifetime of deceit and misery. As Jacob *wrestles* through the night, he slowly begins to see the truth. *Isaac* was never an obstacle to God's promise! *Esau* didn't deserve such treatment. *Mother,* even with all her scheming, cannot be blamed any longer!

By morning Jacob comes to terms with the fact that from his youth, he has been running from and wrestling with only one man - *himself!* The outcome of this *wrestling match* will mark a dividing line between "past failure" and "future greatness."

48

"What is your name?", the heavenly visitor asks. Jacob, in a torrent of emotion, pours out a lifetime in one phrase: *"I am Jacob."* (Gen. 32:27)

Inherent in the reply is the acknowledgement and repentance God has been after for years. Yes, I am the *"heel catcher!"* Yes, I am *"the liar!"* Yes, I am the *"fearful deceiver!"* Yes, I am the *"manipulator!"* Yes I am the *"spoiled self-indulgent child"* who'll destroy anyone who gets in his way! ***Yes, I am Jacob***! With this honest confession, Jacob speaks his last words as a "heel catcher." His next utterance will be that of a "prince."

"…Thy name shall be called no more Jacob but Israel for as a prince hast thou power with God and with men, and hast prevailed… and Jacob called the name of the place Peniel; for I have seen God face to face, and my life is preserved." (Gen. 32:28 – 30)

THE STAFF OF JACOB

The author of Hebrews presents an additional portrait of Jacob as a *man of faith*:

"By faith Jacob, when he was dying, blessed both sons of Joseph; and worshiped, leaning upon the top of his staff." (Heb. 11:21)

Just prior to the *wrestling match* at *Peniel,* Jacob spoke these words,

"…For with my staff I passed over this Jordan." (Gen. 32:10)

Jacob had a friend, a tried and true companion which remained faithfully at his side through all the seasons of his life, a silent witness to all his sufferings, a quiet presence in his poverty, adversity, and loneliness.

His companion? The *wooden staff* of his earthly pilgrimage *"…with my staff I passed over this Jordan." "He blessed … and worshiped … leaning upon the top of his staff."*

Jacob's staff was to become the constant reminder of the humiliation and weakness destined to become the founda-

49

tion of his ministry. The writer of Hebrews gives a *fourfold portrait* of Jacob as *"dying, blessing, worshiping and leaning."* (Heb. 11:21).

Notice that at the end of Jacob's life, the full *weight* of his ministry rests entirely upon his "staff". Jacob's ability to *bless* others as well as his capacity to *worship* would both flow from a *lifetime of leaning.* The *staff of Jacob* would forever point to his "pilgrim identity." It stood as the daily reminder of his abject dependence upon God. *Jacob's staff* was the second confirming witness against Jacob's independence and self-will. The first was his *limp*!

At *Bethel* Jacob picked up this staff and *walked away.* After his encounter at *Peniel,* he will lean for support the rest of his life. The scripture says:

"When the man saw that he could not overpower him he touched the socket of Jacob's hip so that his hip was wrenched as he wrestled...the sun rose above him as he passed Peniel and he was limping because of his hip. Therefore to this day the Israelites do not eat the tendon attached to the socket of the hip because the socket of Jacob's hip was touched near the tendon." (Gen. 32:29, 30-32)

I believe that Jacob's limp became precious to him. Perhaps the only thing more precious in his life and memory was his "staff." Andrew Jukes points out,

"Jacob, to have God's strength, must lose his own.... The man 'whose hand lays hold' is not a 'prince of God,' until the hollow of his thigh is out of joint. When he is weak, then is he strong."

GRACE, THE ONLY TRUE FOUNDATION
OF BLESSING AND WORSHIP

Notice the two *fruits* proceeding from Jacob's "leaning posture": He *blessed* and he *worshiped.* It was as a result of the brokenness of a lifetime that Jacob would *bless others.* It was from a foundation of "humble dependence" that

Jacob would be able to *worship God* in any meaningful way.

"The man asked him, 'What is your name?' 'Jacob,' he answered. Then the man said your name will no longer be Jacob, but Israel, because you have struggled with God and with men and have overcome." (Gen. 32:22,29)

We must *prevail with God* before *we* can *prevail with men*. *Jacob* the deceiver is dead. *Israel* "the prince" now emerges from a long twilight struggle, "leaning" for support upon a "simple staff". Andrew Jukes concludes:

"Would we be Israels? These are the conditions, — to go over Jordan, and wrestle alone, and be smitten in the fleshly part and lamed, and halting; so shall we have power with God and man; and because so few will submit to this, there are many Jacobs, but few Israels."

As it was with Jacob, so it is with us. We *bless others* only to the degree that we will "lean" our full weight upon the *staff of grace*. We *worship God* "in spirit and in truth" only in so far as we can remember who *He is* and who *we used to be*!

How precious is this final portrait of Jacob. He is *dying;* he is *blessing;* and he is *worshiping;* yet all because he is *"leaning."*

A.B. Simpson concludes:

"...out of the thing that is the hardest, we often may get the greatest blessing... Jacob did not get his answer by struggling. When at last he yielded and fell prostrate at the feet of Him who wrestled with him, then he received the blessing... You have been too strong. You have tried to do too much. You thought you could wring the blessing from Esau, outwit Laban, and now propitiate Esau. You have tried to do things yourself, oh Jacob! Fall a helpless child at My feet, and let Me be your strength, and carry you henceforth."

THE FOURFOLD PROMISE OF BETHEL

Let's return for a moment to the four foundational truths which were reiterated in Jacob's *Tardemah of Utter Grace* - truths that formed the foundation for the healing of his past:

- *Security* - His secure standing in the patriarchal line was reaffirmed. (Gen. 28:13)

- *Hope* - He received his personal promise that the land would be given in perpetuity to he and his descendants. (Gen. 28:13)

- *Influence* - Jacob's fruitfulness was guaranteed to affect all future generations. (Gen. 28:14)

- *Favor* - He received the assurance of God's personal presence for the rest of his life (Gen. 28:15)

The promises of *security, hope, influence,* and *favor* will now become the sacred ingredients of the healing balm used for the redemption of Jacob's past!

THREE POINTS OF GRACE
God and Trust

God answers Jacob's issues of *trust,* not by punishing him, but by continuing over and over to demonstrate His own trustworthiness. Despite Jacob's lapses, God uses the continuity of His own covenant faithfulness as the means of healing the "trust breech" in Jacob's soul.

God and Fear

God approaches the great *fear* of Jacob's life with love. Far from *rejecting* or *abandoning* him because of his sins, God instead reconfirms His covenant love by assuring Jacob of his full acceptance in God's generational plan of redemption! It is perfect love alone that drives out fear. Only the assurance of unconditional acceptance can remove the paralyzing effects of fear.

God and Deception

How did God deal with Jacob's deception? Just as He didn't *punish* him for *mistrust* nor *reject* him for his *fear*, so God didn't *demean* Jacob for his *deception,* rather He transformed him!

God doesn't brand him as *worthless*. In fact, God is the very one who will change Jacob's name so that all men for all time may know that God is a God of patience and loving kindness! Far from *demeaning* or *shaming* Jacob, God confronts him with the question his father had asked years before*: What is your name?* Jacob, now all alone with God and surrounded by the security of God's love and direct presence, finally acknowledges the *mistrust, fear,* and *deception* of a lifetime! *"I am Jacob!"*

OUT OF THE BOAT OF TRUTH INTO AN OCEAN OF GRACE

Jacob's confession is more than a mere forced admission due to strong-armed tactics. It is, rather, a glorious release into the greatest blessing of his life. It has been said, with regard to truth telling, that: "One must fall out of the boat of truth into an ocean of grace." God takes this approach to *truth telling* and immediately grants Jacob the blessing of a new name. No, "I told you so's!" No, "If you ever do this again!" No, "You're not worthy of another minute of my time!" Rather, Jacob's lifetime issues are answered by the blessing and goodness of the Lord. *Trust issues* are healed through God's own demonstrable trustworthiness. *Fear issues* are redeemed solely through complete acceptance and love. *Deception* is exposed and transformed by the God of truth as He blesses, not demeans His servant!

DO YOU HAVE A PAST?

You do have a past, don't you? Is there any part of it you wish God would fully redeem? Your sins, whatever their nature and wherever they have led, are also, at root, issues of *trust, fear,* and *deception.* Here's the good news: God is still in the restoring business today. That's what Jacob's

Tardemah of Utter Grace is all about! God has a track record of trustworthiness with regard to you. He has great love and acceptance to offer you. He also has a visitation of grace that can redeem every ruined harvest of your past.

"...and I will restore to you the years that the locust hath eaten, the cankerworm and the caterpillar, and the palmer worm..." (Joel 2:25)

This historic promise to God's people does not promise the impossible, namely *the rewinding of time* in order to properly relive your past life again. What God is talking about, however, is the *restoration* of the "harvests" of those wasted years! The years are gone forever, and with them all the failed harvests they represent. We must grieve the loss of *those* harvests! What God offers is a new and *future* promise of *fruitfulness.* God is able to cause your once barren ground to produce so much in one year, as to surpass all the "harvests" of your lost years put together! What a gracious word of hope!

QUESTIONS FOR REFLECTION

- Jacob was a "passive aggressive, controller." Do you try to control people and things so that situations will work out the way you want them to?
- Jacob wasted decades of "nervous energy" worrying about the fulfillment of a promise that was *already his*! Are you exhausting yourself in stress and anxiety trying to "earn" a blessing God has already promised?
- Jacob reaped consequences in his life due to his deceptiveness. Can you see some of the negative consequences you have brought upon yourself through your own sin?
- Jacob's life was an intricate web of *sin* and *grace.* Yet, his life concluded with twelve sons who would become the twelve tribes, of which one, Judah, would eventually carry on the lineage of the Messiah! It all worked out in the end! Do you have confidence that God will work everything out for you?

As you prepare to pray again, open yourself completely to Him and believe for a complete restoration of your past! Let's be totally honest about our wasted years, knowing that He will always *bless us* if we choose to walk in the light. God offers you the possibility of a bright future no matter where you've been. Why not take Him up on it? From this day forward, *your future is more important than your past!*

A PRAYER FOR A *TARDEMAH* OF UTTER GRACE

"Heavenly Father, I surrender to Your love. I yield to the safety of Your presence. I confess my mistrust and renounce my fears. I acknowledge that I have selfishly met my own needs on my own terms. Forgive my controlling behaviors. I renounce all strongholds of darkness and deception in my life. Please open the floodgates of grace and acceptance to me. Reveal Your glory and heal all my self-inflicted wounds. Remove all curses from my life and family line. Restore the lost harvests of my past. Give me a fruitful life from this day forward."

In Jesus' name.

CHAPTER FIVE

Three *Tardemahs,* One Outpouring

"Look among the nations! Observe! Be astonished! Wonder! Because I am doing something in your days - you would not believe if you were told." (Hab. 1:5)

The three *tardemah*s we have studied together will find a broader application in this chapter.

THREE *TARDEMAHS* IN REVIEW:

Let's review and highlight some of the distinct characteristics of our three *tardemah*s, and then move from "local" *interpretation* to "global" *application.*

THE *TARDEMAH* OF UNKNOWING

The *Tardemah of Unknowing* addresses deeply personal life longings: impossible needs which can be named and met only by God Himself.

THE *TARDEMAH* OF DIVINE DESTINY

The *Tardemah of Divine Destiny* concerns the *life words* God has given and our legitimate need for their reconfirmation. This visitation deals also with the impartations necessary to bring "life words" to pass.

THE *TARDEMAH* OF UTTER GRACE

The *Tardemah of Utter Grace* points us back to the faulty root systems of our unredeemed pasts. Here we encounter a God whose goal is always full and complete restoration without respect of persons

God is a God of balance. He loves a "just weight," especially when dealing with the distribution of His visitations. God, in three portraits of *tardemah,* addresses every aspect of life – *past, present, and future.*

ARE YOU READY FOR A KAIROS?

To underscore the sovereign nature of divine *tardemah*s, let's for a moment consider the very nature of revival.

The first point that must be made in any study of revival is simply that "revival is wholly from God." We can never force God's hand into a sovereign season of refreshing. Acts 1:6,7 declares:

"When they therefore were come together, they asked of him, saying, Lord, wilt though at this time restore again the kingdom to Israel? And He said unto them, it is not for you to know the times or the seasons, which the Father hath put in His own power."

We glean from this passage a very important truth relative to the absolute control of God in *tardemah* seasons of revival.

In Acts1:6, 7, Christ speaks concerning two distinct and separate elements of time, namely, *times* and *seasons*. Two Greek words are in view here, they are: *chronos, (times), and kairos (seasons).*

Greek scholar Kenneth Wuest defines their individual meanings:

"Chronos speaks of time contemplated simply as such, the succession of moments." (Word Studies in Greek New Testament, Vol. II, pg. 30)

Chronos time speaks of *sequential time* as experienced in seconds, minutes, hours, days, months, and years. Simply stated, our *chronos* is what we would call the mundane "nine-to-five;" the "times of our lives," the moments that make up all the time we spend on this earth.

Kairos, however, the word translated *seasons* in our King James Bible, is defined as:

"The joints or articulations of the times, epoch making periods when all that has been maturing through long ages comes to a head in grand and decisive events which constitute the close of one period, and the beginning of another." (Ibid. pg. 30)

This then is revival, i.e., a sovereign *kairos season* conjoining with a prepared *chronos people*.

Simply stated, God alone has absolute control over both *times* and *seasons*!

We cannot cause the wind to blow but we can set our sails. We can never control the waves but we can watch, wait and ride them when they come.

It is a chief characteristic of *tardemah*s that they are impossible to stage. They are sovereign *seasons* proceeding directly from the hand of God.

THREE GLOBAL THEMES FOR THE BODY OF CHRIST
THE TARDEMAH OF UNKNOWING:
HEALING FOR IMPOSSIBLE CASES

Globally, I believe the Lord is about to release a new anointing, the character of which will involve the healing, deliverance, and utter transformation of those who suffer with *impossible conditions*. Some examples, both emotionally and physically, are: *unhealed rape wounds*, *incest wounds*, extreme *emotional trauma*, *ungrieved grief* of every kind, impossible *physical conditions*, unrelenting physical pain, etc.

These represent the areas I believe will be impacted by God's love and mercy. During worship services we will begin to witness an increased environment of God's *glory* that will miraculously bathe and release the inner recesses of the soul, as well as bringing deliverance to chronic physical bondages.

Many of God's people have been following a "recovery process." Through counseling, authentic transformation has been experienced, yet the *healing process* is quite different from the *miraculous nature* of the *Tardemah of Unknowing*.

Such a visitation is more of an *inexplicable intervention* than it is a *deliberate process* over time.

EITHER/OR OR BOTH/AND

The mindset of our present recovery culture might view such *miracle talk* as *magical thinking*. Such *tardemah talk* might sound to some like "pie in the sky" hopes that could lead one into a denial of the healing process. Yet, such an either/or impasse is unnecessary.

We've already mentioned that *chronos time* embodies the *process end* of living, whereas *kairos seasons*, speak of *tardemah interventions* which are the seal of divine visitation in every age.

Let me also mention an important word regarding the moving of God's Holy Spirit. Some woundings are so deep that we should not be surprised if their release is accompanied by emotion, whether expressed in tears or in laughter.

No one would deny a Nazi camp survivor an hour of uncontrollable weeping as they lay before God experiencing His love and grace! Nor would we deny such a soul an hour of laughter granted by God as He more thoroughly cleanses the complex woundings of the human heart. Doesn't it seems strange that some Christians in our time consider it *unbiblical* for tormented souls to express joy or relief when they are miraculously delivered by God?

Let's prepare *our* hearts and pray that God will pour out such healing mercies upon our needy world! The *Tardemah of Unknowing*, God's healing for impossible cases, is on the way!

THE TARDEMAH OF DIVINE DESTINY:
THE RECONFIRMATION AND FULFILLMENT OF LIFE WORDS.

"For as the rain and snow come down from heaven, and do not return there without watering the earth, and making it bear and sprout, and furnishing seed to the sower and bread to the eater; so shall my word be which goes forth from my mouth; it shall not return to me empty, without accomplishing what I desire, and without succeeding in the matter for which I sent it." (Isa. 55:10,11)

"Heaven and earth will pass away, but God's word will never pass away!" Notice this text states that the promise of God always accomplishes that for *which it is sent*. The *logos*, the entire corpus of Biblical revelation, as well as, all *rhema words*, personal life words prompted by the Holy Spirit, *will come to pass!*

Rain produces harvests. *God's word* in any form always produces sovereign results! Let's apply the *Tardemah of Divine Destiny* at its "global level," and see what kind of harvest we will soon encounter .

GOD ANOINTS WHAT HE APPOINTS

The *Tardemah of Divine Destiny* has to do with the reconfirmation of prophetic "life words," in addition to, providing the corresponding impartations necessary to fulfill them.

Romans 1:16 states:

"For I am not ashamed of the gospel, for it is the power of God for salvation to every one who believes..."

Notice God's *power* is always married to His *purpose*. Paul tells us that the simple gospel story has behind it all the resources of omnipotence! God's power is always and only associated with His promise.

It may sound basic, but "God anoints what He appoints." His power and favor are always associated with the "life words" He has given.

FANTASY VERSUS REALITY

God blesses the *visions* He gives, not the *fantasies* we invent.

I once prayed for a woman in a prayer line. As soon as I touched her hand, I knew that she was laboring under unrealistic expectations. Since I was standing in front of hundreds of people, I wanted to be gracious as well as obedient.

I began by saying that God loved her very much and, because of this, He was about to replace some of her hopes and expectations with new ones He would surely bless and fulfill. Well, she didn't respond too well to that suggestion!

I mention her story simply because it is typical of people who cherish humanly contrived *fantasies* above true *prophetic promises*.

Over dinner that evening the pastor told me her story. He said that when she walked up and stood in the prayer line, the entire church staff perked up to hear what I would pray. Evidently she had taken a fancy to a certain young pastor and was *believing she received him*, whether he liked it or not! *He did not!*

The young man had no interest in her, yet she persisted in her misguided *fantasies* and, for all I know, is still *believing she receives* something she'll never have! She had a *fantasy*, a projection of her own imagination, not a *word* from God!

God fulfills His *promises*, never our *fantasies*. *True expectations* that come from God will always be fulfilled in their season.

In the *Tardemah of Divine Destiny* soon to come upon the body of Christ, we will witness the fire of God coming in great mercy to *burn up* the *wood, hay, and stubble* of "human fantasies," while purifying the *gold* and *silver* of "true prophetic expectation."

In the *Tardemah of Divine Destiny*, God will consume our "fantasies" and fulfill our true "life words."

A SEASON OF IMPARTATION

We have pointed out the difference between the two Greek words *chronos* and *kairos*. *Chronos* speaks of our normal nine-to-five, while *kairos* speaks of the extraordinary moments in life when the divine intersects the common. When a *"kairos,"* occurs (and a *Tardemah of Divine Destiny* is a *kairos*) God also bequeaths power to fulfill the *life words* He has given!

Prophetic promises are true the *moment* they are spoken; yet the impartation of negligible power needed to bring them to pass is often delayed for years.

For instance, David's first anointing with oil as Israel's future king was characterized by an immediate impartation of God's presence which never left him, whereas others such as Abraham had to wait years before experiencing their *kairos* fulfillment and corresponding empowerments.

Abraham and Sarah had to be *empowered* with the necessary strength to conceive Isaac. They waited for years exploring every human avenue of fruitfulness, yet to no avail. God imparted His power at a moment chosen and in accordance with His own will. So it will be for you and for so many others in the near future!

Take heart. The coming revival will be an outpouring of God's power for both *reconfirmation* and *impartation*!

THE TARDEMAH OF UTTER GRACE:
THE REDEMPTION OF IMPOSSIBLE PASTS

"Let the quantity of thy sins be the measure of thy repentance" —Isaac Bargrave

"See now that I, even I am he, and there is no God with me; I kill, and I make alive; I wound, and I heal; neither is there any that can deliver out of my hand" (Deut. 32:39)

In chapter four we introduced Jacob's *Tardemah of Utter Grace*. Now we will turn from its local "interpretation" to its "global application." God is getting ready to redeem *impossible pasts*! The question with God is never *"Can He restore?"*, but rather *"will He restore?"*.

Do you have an unredeemed past? If you have experienced "moral failure" of any kind, then there are certainly those once present in your life who will never *trust* you again. There are those who will never be able to bear the *thought* of you. There are even others who will never be able to hear your *voice* proclaiming the word of God again! There are also those who may never be able to *look you in the eye* without Technicolor® images of your past sin flashing across the screen of their minds. The question is: *Is God one of them?*

GOD S LONG LIST

From the Garden of Eden to the present, God has had an "unbroken chain" of "broken links" - men and women who after years at the "mills of sin," return to His work and are fruitful, though chastened and limping for life. The list of the *righteous* is short compared to God's *"long list:"* *Abraham* the adulterer, *Moses* the murderer, *Samson* the fornicator, *David* the murderous adulterer, *Jonah* the rebellious prophet, *Peter* the betrayer, and the list goes on (*your name here* _____).

Deuteronomy 32:39 the above verse, reminds us where we are to turn when dealing with topics as important as *restoration*. We are to *go to God*! It is God who "mends", and God alone who "heals." ***"For he maketh sore, and bindeth up; he woundeth and His hands make whole."*** (Job 5:18) It is God who "sets up one" and "puts down another." (I Sam. 2:6 – 8, Hos. 6:1) The God who alone can "kill" and "make alive" has the only opinion in the universe that should matter to "the fallen." Are you on God's "long list?"

WEEPING WITHOUT A WITNESS

George Swinnock once wrote, "He grieves truly that weeps without a witness." God knows when a heart is truly broken. God knows when the olives are pressed. God knows when His grapes have been crushed. God knows when the grain has been beaten and winnowed. God alone knows the bones He Himself has broken! He who *marked* Jacob for life knows who is truly broken before Him. God always has mercy for those who "weep without a witness."

THE WAGES OF SIN

Sin, in any form, is an abomination to God. Sin stains the conscience, betrays sacred associations, ruins our moral influence in the world, and defiles all that is holy. John Bunyan rightly said, "Sin is the dare of God's justice, the rape of His mercy, the jeer of His patience, the slight of His power, and the contempt of His love."

Whenever a leader sins, he drops a stone into the moral waters surrounding him, whose ripples go on indefinately! Place a tarred hand on a Rembrandt then try to restore it to its original condition! Paste two pieces of paper together, let them dry, then separate them without doing damage to either. Impossible! You're right, it is *impossible* with men!

That's why God is just about to move! Only the God of the "impossible" can redeem "impossible pasts."

As admittedly horrifying as sin is, *what's done is done and cannot be undone*! Even God can't *change* your past, but that does not mean He cannot *redeem it*! In the final analysis with regard to restoration to ministry, there is only one formula that stands the test of time. *"When God says yes, nobody can say no."*

FOUR CHANNELS, ONE RIVER

Where does someone begin when it's too late to begin from the beginning? One fact we can all agree upon is that *restoration is impossible apart from a repentant heart.*

I believe there are four attitudes or "channels" we must dig if we are to be prepared to receive the full impact of the restorative river God is just about to send.

Channel Number One:

- *The Channel of Uninhibited Confession.* The restoration of our pasts will be impossible apart from absolute and uninhibited *confession* of sin.

Transparency always draws *cleansing* from God and *mercy* from others. Puritan theologian John Trapp once said, *"God puts away many in anger for their supposed goodness, but not any at all for their confessed badness."*

A visitor seeking to console the dying Thomas Hooker said, "Sir, you are going to receive the reward of your labor." To which Hooker replied, "No brother, I'm going to receive mercy." We need God's mercy if our pasts are to be fully redeemed! *Grace* is getting what we *don't* deserve while *mercy* is not getting what we *do* deserve. We need mercy! There is no sin greater than God's capacity to forgive. Thomas Horton once wrote, "The sin which is not too great to be forsaken is not too great to be forgiven." If you're willing to walk in *abject honesty* and *uninhibited confession* with trusted others, God's great river of restoration will cleanse your past.

Channel Number Two:

- *The Channel of Accepted Responsibility.* God's torrents of restoration will surge *around* and leave *utterly dry* and *barren* all who refuse to take *personal responsibility* for their own sin. God only wants to hear about *you.* He knows everything and more about *them.* What is *your* part? What is *your* responsibility? How did *you* contribute to the situation? Be as candid as Jacob when he met God face to face. Accept personal blame for your sins and you will be able to embrace the mighty river of grace which alone can restore your past.

Channel Number Three:

- *The Channel of Humility and Accountability.* All of nature testifies to the importance of shared *soil, sunlight, rain, and fresh air* if life is to exist and growth is to be sustained. The *plants* have roots, the *trees* have roots, and *you* need roots, little flower! God has created us with the need to live *interdependently.* You need people, and people need you! No man or woman is an island. *Isolation* is the very essence of hell, while *chosen relationships* of safety are the very essence of heaven. Whenever we humble ourselves and choose to be accountable to the "Godly relationships" in our lives then floodgates of restoration are opened to us! Open the channel of *humility and accountability,* and the withered roots of your past will be nourished and restored.

Channel Number Four:

- *The Channel of Entitlement-free Living.* When a heart is truly broken it makes no demands. Only God knows the true condition of a human heart. However, when a heart is truly broken, it will set no conditions for restoration. When we *argue, wrestle, protest,* and *demand* we demonstrate to God and those around us that repentance has not yet ripened in our hearts. Drop your demands and excuses. Open the channel of *entitlement-free living*, and God's river of grace will cleanse your past and restore hope.

There is a great restoration coming upon the world, a grand redemption for "leader" and "laymen" alike. God has many soldiers in His army. Many are wounded soldiers with invaluable training and experience. Tens of millions of them will soon be restored to active duty. God has invested too much in them to leave them where they are.

The choice is yours! Become a person of *uninhibited confession,* one who embraces *personal responsibility*, and actively pursues interdependent relationships of *accountability*. Become like Jacob and surrender your *demands*, then you will be *ready for the river*.

Give God your past, and in return, He'll give you a glorious new future.

QUESTIONS FOR REFLECTION:

- God has a vision which embraces your *past*, your *present,* and your *future*. Do you? Which of these three are you most reluctant to surrender to Him?
- When you consider the *past*, the *present* and *future,* which do you feel you have a special anointing to address?
- Will you begin to pray at a "global level" for God to: (1) heal impossible cases, (2) reconfirm and fulfill "impossible destinies," and (3) to redeem "impossible pasts."

CHAPTER SIX

God, Tardemah, and You

The primary responsibility of the preacher is threefold: to *tell them what you're going to tell them*, to *tell them*, and then to *tell them what you told them.*

In the *introduction* "I told you what I was going to tell you." In *chapters two through five*, "I told you." Now, in this *final chapter*, "I'll tell you what I told you." After which we'll offer a word of warning concerning the Devil's *four strategies* against God's *three tardemahs*.

THE THREE DIMENSIONS OF HUMAN NEED

As sinful human beings, any *redemption* or *restoration* offered us must embrace all "three dimensions" of human existence: the *past,* the *present, and* the *future.* We've examined the fact that God's grace extends to our *past,* Jacob's *Tardemah of Utter Grace,* our *present,* Adam's *tardemah of unknowing*, and our future, Abraham's *tardemah of divine destiny.*

Our *past* embraces the world of *memory,* our *present* the world of *realities*, and our *future* the world of *promise.* If we want to be practical people, we must prepare to allow God to impact all three.

READY OR NOT, HERE I COME!

Nothing you can *say* or *do*, whether good or evil, can ever *hasten* or *hinder* a *tardemah season.* It is important that we embrace this fact! Consider the four seasons. They *come when they come* and they *go when they go.* They are, as in the case of winter, often *merciless* in their advent and *utterly blind* to our personal concerns. They take no account of our *comfort* or *opinion.* We must adapt to *seasons. Seasons* will never adapt to us!

The three *tardemah seasons* we've studied are coming upon the world, whether we are individually prepared or not! If we *prepare ourselves*, we can "catch the wave" when it comes and ride it safely to the shore. If we are indifferent to such *seasonal realities,* we will be "strewn on the beach!" *Intercession, worship,* our *obedience to the Word,* all are necessary components of the spiritual life, yet they can neither *hasten* nor *hinder* the sovereign hand of God in revival. The best we can do is to *prepare* our hearts while waiting patiently for seasons to change.

"NOAH" CONTROL OVER THE ARK

The ark of Noah is an apt symbol of the posture we must adopt as the waters of revival begin to rise around us. Notice the ark had no *oars,* no *rudder,* no *sail,* and certainly no *engine*! Noah and his family were "sealed in" with "Noah" control over the ark. The "ark of safety" rose as the waters of destruction rose. God brought *deliverance* through *destruction*! They were not in control of anything, neither are you. God and God alone brought the *rain.* God and God alone *broke up the fountains of the great deep* and only God could *sustain* them through the turbulent flood! The waters of blessing that lifted the ark were waters of destruction to the ungodly. There will not be *two visitations* – one to *judge* and one to *bless.* There will be only *one!* It will be *judgement* to the unprepared yet *salvation* to God's elect. Noah faithfully built the boat in *preparation,* but he could not make it rain! You and I have no control over the rising waters. We can only hang on and enjoy the ride.

GOD, TARDEMAH, AND YOU

"From now on I will tell you of new things, of hidden things unknown to you. They are created now, and not long ago; you have not heard of them before today. So you cannot say, 'Yes, I knew of them.'" (Is. 48:6,7)

God is a God who does "new things" – things that have never been done before! Dick Mills, in his excellent booklet *The New Wave of the Holy Spirit* (Harrison House, 1983, pp. 8-18), offers a list of ten distinctive *signposts* that serve as indicators that God is doing a "new thing" in the earth. These will serve as ten practical preparatory steps which must be recognized and embraced if we are to flow with the three *tardemah* seasons soon to come upon us.

SIGNPOST #1 — WE MUST PREPARE FOR THE LOCAL CHURCH TO BECOME THE FOCAL POINT OF WORSHIP.

God is going to point our attention back to our need for deeply rooted relational ties at the local level. *Tardemah seasons*, as glorious as they may be, can never replace our need for *interdependent* connection with a local body of believers.

SIGNPOST #2 — WE MUST PREPARE FOR A NEW EMPHASIS ON EVANGELISM.

The three *tardemah seasons* will impact our *past*, *present* and, *future* only to the end of healing and equipping us for the work of evangelism and soul winning.

SIGNPOST #3 — WE MUST PREPARE FOR A NEW ALERTING TO SPIRITUAL WARFARE

We are currently in the midst of this important season. God will continue to give us new strategies from *heaven* so that we can soundly defeat all the strategies of *hell*.

SIGNPOST #4 — WE MUST PREPARE FOR A NEW CALL TO INTERCESSION.

At the time of this writing, we are in the midst of a mighty revival of prayer and intercession.

SIGNPOST #5 — WE MUST PREPARE FOR A NEW COMMITMENT TO PERSONAL HOLINESS

Dick Mills points out, *"The first wave in the early 20th Century went to extremes regarding dress codes, legalism, and a rigid list of do's and don't's.... Holiness was reduced to an external. The second wave at mid-century swung like a pendulum the other way, taking a passive attitude about world separation and holy living. The new wave will equalize the positions of extreme legalism and extreme permissiveness. Like a pendulum that settles for the middle, it will normalize with an awesome holiness and righteousness befitting the church of the living God."* (p. 12)

SIGNPOST #6 — WE MUST PREPARE FOR NEW MODES OF WORSHIP

Again at this writing, we are enjoying a virtual explosion of new modes of worship, which will only increase over time.

SIGNPOST #7— WE MUST PREPARE FOR A NEW SURGE OF THE MIRACULOUS

Dick Mills states, *"Moses was told twice by the Lord, "Go back and face the evil world system. I'm going to multiply my signs, wonders, and miracles in the land." (Exodus 7:3; 11:9.) ... We can expect the church age, which began with a burst of the supernatural evidences, to end full circle at the Second Coming. The church will once again have apostolic purity, power, and productivity."* (pp. 14, 15)

SIGNPOST #8 — WE MUST PREPARE FOR A NEW WAVE OF DELIVERANCES DURING WORSHIP

He continues, *"Many of the greatest miracles in the future will occur during worship. There will be a total restoration of alcoholics, homosexuals, rape and incest victims, people who have been violently abused, cancer victims, and others who are injured in spirit, soul, and body. The psalmist, David, spoke of the Lord's power and glory being seen in the sanctuary. (Ps. 63:1,2)"* (p. 17)

SIGNPOST #9 — WE MUST PREPARE FOR THE COMING WAVE OF PERSECUTION

He adds, *"As the Holy Spirit sweeps the world, inundating the church with His presence, the enemy will be stirred with a malignant hatred that will bring persecution to believers worldwide... The persecution of the future will be a fulfillment of Psalm 2:1-4... The main thrust of the coming persecution will be verbal abuse against the righteous. Look for sarcasm, ridicule, and mockery.... Job 5:21 says the Lord will hide us "from the scourge of the tongue." Psalm 31:20 says the Lord will keep us "secretly in a safe place from the strife of tongues.""* (pp. 18-20)

SIGNPOST #10 — WE MUST PREPARE FOR A NEW WAVE OF UNITY IN THE CHRISTIAN CHURCH.

He concludes, *"While the world is falling apart, the Christians are falling together. Unbelief is an isometric that will cause believers to toughen up. Jesus' prayer for unity in John 17:21 will be answered. ...The one thing that will unite Christian believers is love – love for the Lord Jesus, love for His people, and love for His rhema promises."* (pp. 22-23)

A TARDEMAH INVENTORY

- Are you currently allowing *God* to address all three dimensions of your life: the world of *memory* (the past), the world of *realities* (the present), and the world of *promise* (the future).
- Which do *you* spend the most time addressing? Your *memories*, your *promises* or your *realities*?
- Are you willing to be "sealed up in the ark," surrendering all control of your life and circumstances to God?
- Are you willing to pray and practically prepare for God to turn your focus to ministry in the "local church" with a new passion for "evangelism," "spiritual warfare," "intercession," "personal holiness," "worship," the "miraculous," and "deliverance," while standing strong in the midst of "persecution?"

It is proper and fitting that we should conclude our study with a brief examination of what hell has planned in an attempt to counter God's blessing! Puritan theologian Vavasor Powell once wrote, "Satan doth not like God, warn before he strikes." This is true, but we have the Holy Spirit to warn us! It's best that we take a moment to watch Satan, for he surely watches us. In order to be prepared for everything, we will now examine four of Satan's "counterfeit tardemahs!"

SLEEP AND ITS COUNTERFEITS

"Sin is like the little serpent aspis, which stings men,

whereby they fall into a pleasant sleep, and in that sleep die." —Swinnock

As with everything created by God, Satan always has his corresponding counterfeits. It should come as no surprise then that the Bible records the fact of counterfeit *tardemah*s!

FOUR KINDS OF SLEEP

The word *tardemah* is also used in scripture to speak of *unholy slumber*, sleep which makes us vulnerable to satanic attack. Just as God has designed sovereign *tardemah* "seasons" of blessing, so Satan seeks to bring his "counterfeit sleep" into our lives. These four kinds of counterfeit sleep always represent the most subtle threat to revival in any age. They are:

- The sleep of "*escape*"
- The sleep of "*presumption*"
- The sleep of "*transgression*"
- The sleep of "*error*"

JONAH AND THE SLEEP OF ESCAPE

"But, Jonah was gone down into the sides of the ship; and he lay, and was fast asleep." (Jonah 1:5)

What a curious instance of *deep sleep*. Willen A. Van Gemeren explains:

> *"The use of tardemah in Jonah 1:5,6 may be ironic, pointing to a prophet who fell asleep not in order to establish contact with God, but to escape it."* (Dictionary of Old Testament Theology and Exegesis, Vol. III, Zondervan, 1997, pg. 1057)

I believe that the great reality and power of addiction in our culture parallels Jonah's express desire to *escape* through sleep. When we seek to evade the realities and responsibilities of life through any form of *mood altering* slumber, we risk the danger of awaking to find ourselves, like Jonah, *hidden*, *isolated* and *running* from God!

Our families and friends are all too often forced to take on the role of Jonah's shipmaster who cried:

"What meanest thou, O' sleeper, arise, call upon thy God, ...that we perish not." (Jonah 1:6)

It's time to "wake up" to call upon God and turn from the false *sleep of escape!*

We make ourselves vulnerable to Satan's greatest bondages when we sleep to God's will, God's call, and God's word! Such a *sleep of escape* proves a contradiction even to non-believers who ask: *"Why hast thou done this."* (Jonah 1:10). Satan watches over all those who presently slumber in *escapism.*

Notice also the familiar theme in Jonah's steps toward his *sleep of escape:*

"He went down to Joppa...He entered the ship...paid the fare...and went down into it...but, when Jonah was gone down into the sides of the ship; he lay, and was fast asleep

He went down into the sea...then down into the whale's belly." (Jonah 1:3,5; 2:15,17)

When we run from God in order to evade the realities and responsibilities of life we always go *down!* The sleep of *escape* always leads *down* and *away* from God's blessing. Notice also that when we run from God, we always *pay the fare* and *never reach our destination*! So it is with the reality of addiction in any of its forms. We pay with our lives to sleep a sleep of utter isolation and fruitlessness.

Let's heed the counsel of the apostle Paul and:

"Awake to righteousness and sin not...." (I Cor. 15:34)

SISERA AND THE SLEEP OF PRESUMPTION

"Then Jael, Heber's wife took a nail of the tent, and took an hammer in her hand...and smote the nail into his temples, and fastened it into the ground: for he was fast asleep and weary so he died." (Judges 4:21)

What penetrating words, "*...he was fast asleep...so he died.* To *presume* means, "to take upon one's self without leave or warrant: to dare, to expect or assume, especially with confidence, to go beyond what is right or proper."

Presumption in *conduct* is what we call *audacity*! Unfortunately we have all at one time or another been guilty of *presumption*.

Sisera, the enemy of God's people, drove in a panic over the hills to Zaanaim. He trusted in his countless number of armed men. He trusted the weight of King Jabin's chariots. Because of such "presumption," God delivered him into the hands of Jael. Sisera's own "sleep of presumption" would unite him with the prepared destruction of the Canaanite peoples. Sisera was an enemy of God's people and purposes. He was a Canaanite ruler, a tyrant typical of all persecutors in every age.

He opposed God's work until *"the very stars in their courses fought against Sisera."* (Judges 5:20) Creation itself opposes the sin of presumption. The presumptuousness of a lifetime led Sisera into Jael's tent where at her feet he fell into one last sleep – a *"sleep of presumption."*

Sadly, many of us have been treading on dangerous ground; we have been *presuming upon God*! We *presume* that there is no end to mercy. We *presume* that our little idiosyncrasies are not really sin. We *presume* that God thinks as we do. We *presume* that God "grades on the curve." *Presumption is indeed the sleep of fools.*

Are you presuming upon God today? Did you know that you open yourself to Satan's cruelest intentions when you sleep the sleep of *presumption*? Listen to the Psalmist:

"These things you have done, and I kept silent; You thought that I was just like you; I will reprove you, and state the case in order before your eyes." (Ps. 50:21).

Let's not presume any more upon the grace of God. Let's not waste another minute in a counterfeit sleep that would lead us "beyond that which is right or proper." Presumption, and the sleep it produces, brought a swift end to Sisera and his works. We would do well to heed this warning!

"…it is high time to awake out of sleep…." (Rom. 13:11)

SAMSON AND THE SLEEP OF TRANSGRESSION

"And she made him sleep upon her knees...and he awoke out of his sleep and said, I will go out as at other times before, and shake myself. And he wist not that the Lord was departed from him." (Judges 16:19,20)

Samson, the great judge of Israel, slept a costly sleep. His story and example are clear for all to see.

Samson was a great leader, yet he fell into a lifestyle of "transgression." To transgress means "to pass over a limit or boundary." Transgression is an "infringement" or "violation of a law, duty, or command."

I would add to these definitions the words: "over time." It is only "over time" that a seed flowers enough to reveal its true character. It is only "over time" that the true harvests of our lives appear. It is only "after awhile," as one sleeps a *"sleep of transgression,"* that Ecclesiastes 8:11 becomes a reality:

"Because sentence against an evil work is not executed speedily, therefore the heart of the sons of men is fully set in them to do evil."

Just as Jonah went *down* in his "sleep of escape," so Samson runs red light after red light, until he finally crashes into the inevitable wall of sin's consequences!

When a leader hits bottom, he has usually been falling for a long time! God is gracious. He protects us even in inappropriate seasons of slumber. We sleep the sleep of *"escape,"* and He sends grace. We sleep the sleep of *"presumption,"* and He shows mercy.

God gave Samson opportunity after opportunity to repent of his sin, but he would not! Stepping over the line one too many times, the great judge of Israel slept a *sleep of transgression* from which he would never fully wake.

Satan, after shearing Samson's locks of influence and power, quickly led him off to the grinding mill of slavery, bound and blind!

Please don't fall prey to the deep sleep of *transgression.* Repent now. Let God's gracious work of restoration begin!

77

"Awake thou that sleepest and Christ shall give thee light." (Eph. 5:14)

SAUL AND THE SLEEP OF ERROR

"David took the spear and the cruse of water from Saul's bolster;...and no man saw it, nor knew it, neither awaked: for they were asleep: because a deep sleep from the Lord was fallen upon them." (I Sam. 26:2)

Saul, the first king of Israel, is the man spoken of here. Saul's error began the day he misread the praises of some young women in Israel.

"And it came to pass as they came, when David was returned from the slaughter of the Philistine, that the women came out of all cities of Israel, singing and dancing, to meet king Saul...and said, Saul hath slain his thousands, and David his tens of thousands." (I Sam. 18:6,7)

The passage ends with eight tragic words:

"And Saul eyed David from that day forward." (I Sam. 18:9)

The seed of error was sown! The error Saul embraced about David would lead him into a deep *"sleep of error."* Twice God would deliver a sleeping Saul into David's hand, (I Sam. 24:1-22; 26:5-25) and twice judgment would not be visited upon him because of David's gracious conduct.

Will we ever realize the depth of Christ's love for us and the depth of Satan's hatred? How often have we slept a deep sleep of *escape, presumption, transgression, or error* while judgment hung just above our heads!

Saul was wrong to mistrust David. Yet he found a following ready to assist him. A *simple error* led Saul to the place where in flagrant error he now fights the living God! Are you in error? Are you resisting the will of God for your life? Do you have a distorted picture of *God, others,* and *yourself* ?

78

There are times in life when you can find yourself "sincere" yet "sincerely wrong!" Saul experienced this. He received one *seed* of error into his heart, only to allow a full *harvest* of error which would poison the remaining years of his life.

When we sleep the *sleep of error*, our slumber is the only thing that blinds us to the destruction standing just above our heads! Satan's counterfeits are powerful. So we must identify and then resist them! The devil is an attractive artist. He paints sin in very attractive colors.

QUESTIONS FOR REFLECTION

- Do you frequently "act out" in mood altering behaviors in order to evade the responsibilities of life? This is the *sleep of escape*.
- Are you currently assuming you're right about most things? Do you imagine that God approves of most everything you do? This is the *sleep of presumption*.
- Are you currently living a lifestyle of sin, constantly running "red lights," yet imagining you are exempt from consequences? This is the *sleep of transgression*
- Are you currently nursing a deception in your heart concerning God, others or yourself? Do "reality distortions" find their way easily into your thinking? This is a *sleep of error*.

"The Christian soldier must avoid two evils – he must not faint or yield in the time of fight, and after a victory he must not wax insolent and secure. When he has overcome, he is so to behave himself as though he were presently again to be assaulted. For Satan's temptations, like the waves of the sea, do follow one in the neck of the other." —George Downame

A PRAYER OF DELIVERANCE FROM COUNTERFEIT SLEEP

Lord, I humble myself before You. I confess and renounce my utter blindness concerning my own sin. Show me the areas where I am attempting to *escape* reality through addictive behaviors. Uncover and remove each false assumption I treasure as the truth. Let presumption and its roots be exposed and removed from my life. Impress upon me the reality of sin's consequences. Deliver me from a heart unmoved by transgression. Deliver me from deception, distortion, and every perversion of truth I currently embrace. I renounce my desire to *escape*. I confess the sin of *presumption*. I acknowledge my *transgressions*. Deliver me from *error* and lead me into your truth.

In Jesus' name.

* * * * *

To book Dr. Craig Johnson for speaking engagements, or to order his album *Valley of Vision*, please contact him at:

Bethel Christian Fellowship
5310 Dewey Drive, Suite P
Agora Hills, CA 91301
818-889-7215 (ph)
818-889-7253 (fx)
BETHELCF@aol.com